D0072595

POWER
AND
RESTRAINT

POWER
and
RESTRAINT

The Moral Dimension of Police Work

Howard S. Cohen
and
Michael Feldberg

PRAEGER

New York
Westport, Connecticut
London

Library of Congress Cataloging-in-Publication Data

Cohen, Howard, 1944–
    Power and restraint : the moral dimension of police work / Howard
S. Cohen, Michael Feldberg.
      p.   cm.
    Includes bibliographical references and index.
    ISBN 0–275–93856–5 (alk. paper). — ISBN 0–275–93857–3 (pbk. : alk.
paper)
    1. Police ethics. 2. Law enforcement—United States—Moral and
ethical aspects. 3. Police ethics—Case studies. 4. Law
enforcement—United States—Moral and ethical aspects—Case studies.
I. Feldberg, Michael, 1943– . II. Title.
HV7924.C64   1991
174'.93632'0973—dc20   90–28100

British Library Cataloguing in Publication Data is available.

Copyright © 1991 by Howard S. Cohen and Michael Feldberg

All rights reserved. No portion of this book may
be reproduced, by any process or technique, without
the express written consent of the publisher.

Library of Congress Catalog Card Number: 90–28100
ISBN: 0–275–93856–5 (hbk.)
      0–275–93857–3 (pbk.)

First published in 1991

Praeger Publishers, One Madison Avenue, New York, NY 10010
An imprint of Greenwood Publishing Group, Inc.

Printed in the United States of America

The paper used in this book complies with the
Permanent Paper Standard issued by the National
Information Standards Organization (Z39. 48–1984).

P

In order to keep this title in print and available to the academic community, this edition
was produced using digital reprint technology in a relatively short print run. This would
not have been attainable using traditional methods. Although the cover has been changed
from its original appearance, the text remains the same and all materials and methods
used still conform to the highest book-making standards.

For Patti and Ruth

Contents

Preface

It is now more than a decade since the authors took their first steps toward understanding the moral dimensions of police work. In 1979, with a grant from the National Endowment for the Humanities, we began designing the Law Enforcement Trainers Institute (LETI), a summer program in humanities for police personnel. We were confident that the collaboration between academic humanists and police professionals could be fruitful. It is safe to say, however, that we did not begin to see how fascinating, complex and truly mutual the intellectual journey would become. In our initial planning of this first summer program, we harbored no illusions that we knew much about police work. Nevertheless, we were cheered by the thought that the police officers and trainers we would work with were at a corresponding disadvantage regarding history, ethics and the world of social thought that was so much on our own horizons. A collaboration in which all parties enter with complementary proclaimed strengths and proclaimed ignorance requires serious trust on all sides if it is to be productive. We are deeply grateful that we could trust, and be trusted by, the countless people of good will who enriched our minds and lives.

Our initial thanks must go the National Endowment for the Humanities and the National Association of State Directors of Law Enforcement Trainers. The former was willing to support our dialog in the humanities with a population that was not in its traditional domain. The latter put its organizational clout behind our idea and made it possible to recruit program participants who had positions of importance in police training across the country. These two organizations were the bedrock of the Law Enforcement Trainers Institute. We could not have done it without them.

The first LETI attracted a really remarkable group of police personnel who were willing to spend six weeks with us learning about ethics, history, culture and the foundations of the Constitution. They also taught us about their own moral concerns and their reactions to ethical problems. Together we were able to find concepts that illuminated police experience in the moral realm. Six weeks is a heavy commitment for busy professionals, and we are grateful that they took it so seriously.

Our thanks must also go to the literally hundreds of trainers, officers and academy personnel who followed that original group in our subsequent seminars. Our teaching, which was also our research, was a process of proposing, discussing and refining cases that made sense to professionals in the field. Their collective, reflective wisdom is the experience that grounded and molded our theories.

Historians and philosophers are accustomed to doing their research in libraries. We did much of ours "on the road." We held our training sessions in Georgia, Arkansas, Oregon, Maryland and New York. We worked with police in California, Nevada, Maine and Massachusetts. In all of these journeys, we were shown great kindness and consideration by the personnel of the agencies that invited us. Police, as a group, have been unfailingly generous to us with their time and energy; we are deeply appreciative.

Our journeys also placed heavy demands on our wives, Patti Cohen and Ruth Feldberg. They have been ever encouraging of our pursuit of this interest and, on occasion, indulgent of our excessive zeal. They have helped us to stay with our project as our careers took various turns. Our debt to them became especially clear to us as this book reached completion.

Our gratitude goes as well to William Geller, Craig B. Fraser, John Kleinig, Hillary Robinette and Saul Touster for their careful reading of and comments on the manuscript. Their suggestions saved us from many errors; those that remain should be charged solely to our account.

Introduction

This book takes its place among a relatively few others in the philosophical study of police ethics. The relative shortage of serious studies of police ethics is surprising, given the American public's long-standing fascination with the moral dimensions of police behavior. Newspapers have for generations made police scandals a front-page staple. American readers, television watchers and moviegoers consume a steady diet of stories depicting police brutality, inefficiency, stupidity, corruption, dereliction of duty, favoritism and discrimination against unpopular groups. Segments of the contemporary general public seem to hold the image that a significant proportion of police officers are lazy, corrupt, intolerant or brutal, and that the moral standards of the ''average'' police officer are pretty low. Put another way, many Americans assume that, at this very moment, a large proportion of their local police officers are down at the doughnut shop, swigging free coffee and chatting with the waitress.

The general public may well retain its fixed moral image of the police, but since the 1970s, social science researchers have been steadily revising our scholarly understanding of police work. As we explain in detail in Chapter 1, social scientists first began to look at the police in the 1950s, and undertook a thorough scrutiny in the late 1960s and 1970s, in the wake of anti-establishment rioting triggered by police/citizen confrontations in the nation's urban ghettos and the conflict between police and anti-Vietnam war demonstrators. What these observers found was that, in reality, police work largely involved routine social service and human relations tasks. Most officers only occasionally engaged in crime fighting or formal enforcement of the criminal law. For this reason, police work tends to involve less use of force and fewer opportunities for corruption than its popular image. Furthermore, compared to their counterparts in many other nations, American police officers are much more civilianized and heavily restrained by law, constitutional limitations, community expectations and traditions in their exercise of authority and power. Although scholarly studies of police officers and their work in the last twenty years have given us reasons to be pleased by the relative restraint with which American police operate, what we have learned about police still raises many serious ethical, legal and constitutional issues worthy of deeper analysis.

This book aspires to define an ethical basis for and standards by which to evaluate American police work. This Introduction describes the way the present authors learned enough about policing to arrive at the ethical standards enunciated in Chapter 3. It also allows us to acknowledge our intellectual debt to those who shared their experiences and insights about police work with us for a decade.

We began our involvement with the study of police ethics in 1979, when the National Endowment of the Humanities provided Boston University with funds to create the Law Enforcement Trainers Institute (LETI), administered by Michael Feldberg. The LETI brought together police-training specialists from across the United States to attend seminars led by academic humanists in constitutional law, police in American history and culture, and police ethics, as well as a seminar in classroom teaching methods.

The original LETI police ethics seminar, "Working Ethics for Police," was jointly taught by Howard Cohen and Elizabeth Barker. Participants studied moral philosophy and police in literature, formulated the most salient moral issues in police work as they had personally experienced it and explored those issues through discussion. Each participant in the seminar also developed a statement of a moral issue and an approach for discussing it that could be integrated into the police training curriculum he was teaching at his home academy.

These first year's efforts allowed us to identify the issues that a group of thoughtful, experienced police officers considered major moral concerns. In the second and third years of the LETI, our concern turned to (1) providing the participants with a vocabulary for expressing the police experience in the language of morality, (2) creating a framework for moral discussion that participants could use with confidence and (3) giving participants practice in leading discussion on ethical issues.[1] At the end of the three-year effort, the LETI police ethics seminar produced a written ethics curriculum that was adopted (with modifications for local conditions) in a handful of police academies around the United States. For example, one participant from a southwestern state used the examples developed at LETI to lead discussions during orientation sessions for spouses of newly recruited state troopers. He wanted the spouses to have a better grasp of the kinds of issues their trooper-spouses would be facing in the course of their careers. Another participant from a municipal police department in a neighboring state developed his department's first full-blown ethics course. A third used it as part of a police science course he was teaching in an upstate New York community college.

Our thinking about how to develop a method for discussing ethical issues with working police officers was further developed and refined when, from 1982 through 1984, the authors were invited by the Institute for the Humanities and Law Enforcement Training (IHLET) of the National Association of State Directors of Law Enforcement Training to teach a series of five-day courses to police-training officers, supervisors and curriculum developers in various cities around the United States. This series of seminars allowed us to travel around the nation, observe the police-training process at various regional and state academies, and learn about the similarities and variations in moral attitudes among police officers and trainers from the various sections of this nation.[2]

For us, LETI and IHLET were instrumental in adding two additional pieces to the existing scholarship on the moral dimensions of police work. First, the hundreds of hours we spent talking to working police officers and trainers (and most trainers are current or former officers) enabled us to engage police practitioners in careful discussion of specific cases. We developed a body of examples of moral issues that were most troubling to the police themselves. Some of the most interesting appear as examples for the reader's analysis in Chapters 4 through 7. By talking through these examples with participants at these seminars, we became able to identify those features of the examples that seemed *morally* significant (as opposed to tactically best or most efficient) for a police officer to consider when he or she was deciding how to handle an incident. Over the years, we came to understand the moral perceptions of police officers better and to design hypothetical incidents that brought those moral considerations to light.

Second, we were able to use the institutes to link the moral judgments police officers made in particular situations with more general theoretical conceptions of moral philosophy. We wanted to connect very general philosophical concepts such as the ''social contract'' with the participants' reasoning about specific cases. Our goal was to find a way to unify the judgments that participants were making about particular moral problems in their own work into a more consistent conception of general standards of good police work.

The eight years that we worked together helping police trainers to develop ethics curricula, providing our own version of ethics training for police recruits and experienced officers, and in talking with literally hundreds of police officers about the moral dimensions of their work have yielded the experience that is the grounding of this book. In those seminars, training sessions and conversations, we were able to formulate, correct and reformulate our understanding of the moral problems that police face in their work. We were able to develop arguments supporting the morally best options for action in certain typical, recurrent and chronically perplexing situations that street police officers face, and have those arguments challenged by officers who had actually faced them. We were able to reformulate our ''Monday morning quarterbacks' '' view to take better account of the practitioners' criticisms. We were able to listen to the moral justifications officers would offer for choosing one course of action over others, raise questions about those justifications, hear the responses and think about the challenges officers posed to each other. When, in the course of this book, the reader encounters phrases such as, ''Our experience with police officers seems to indicate that . . . '' or ''Most officers we have spoken to tell us that . . . ,'' we are referring primarily to what we learned from police officers' structured discussions of scenarios, such as those contained in Chapters 4 through 7 of this book that deal with such issues as excessive force, gratuities and corruption, balancing individual rights with keeping the peace, and sorting through the conflict between, on the one hand, loyalty to colleagues and, on the other, telling the truth under oath about their wrongdoing.

Our work took a step forward in 1986 when we were asked by Wasserman Associates to develop a self-paced learning manual on moral issues in policing through which police recruits could ''teach themselves'' ethics.[3] We realized that a self-paced teaching manual for police recruits, if it could work at all, could not deal extensively with moral theory, but would need to introduce a clear set of moral concepts that recruits could use as a guide for thinking about the problems we identify in the discussion scenarios. This assignment asked us, basically, to design a training manual that would lead police recruits through a ''discussion'' of ethical decision-making at which, very possibly, no instructor or discussion leader would be present, and that a recruit might complete as homework. Finally, we were to be physically separated from the teaching of our program, and this forced us to think more carefully about how to provide a reader with a moral perspective that would illuminate the widest range of moral issues in police work and permit the reader to judge possible responses to particular cases against a broader moral view of what ''good'' police work is.

In the course of this new assignment, we realized that a social contract perspective, emphasizing the duties and responsibilities of public agents, would permit us to accomplish this task. Working from John Locke's *Second Treatise of Civil Government*, which provided much of the theoretical underpinnings for the U.S. Declaration of Independence and Constitution, we generated standards of behavior for those persons whose authority is derived from the citizenry via a hypothetical bargain. Rather than focusing on the scope and limits of citizen obedience or the source of state authority, we asked, ''What responsibilities do governmental officials incur in consequence of accepting the authority to govern?'' Our answer, explored in depth in Chapters 2 and 3, is that governmental officials in general, and police officers in particular, must meet five standards of responsibility, each of which, to some degree, imposes some restraint upon the power officers are given (thus, the title of this book). In a nutshell, these five standards say that police must (1) provide fair access to their services; (2) insure that their power, held and used as a public trust, will not be abused; (3) put the primacy of safety and security of citizens before the unreflective enforcement of law; (4) acknowledge the coordination of governance with other officials in the system; and (5) maintain an attitude of non-partisan objectivity in carrying out their functions. These standards attempt both to define a minimum measure of officer behavior that it would be wrong not to meet as well as to establish moral goals that officers should strive to achieve.

Armed with these standards, it is possible for a police recruit, or

anyone thinking about the moral dimensions of police behavior in mor⁻
ally complex situations, to work through a variety of possible responses
to those situations, and determine better and worse courses of action to
take. Of course, there will be situations in which there can be no entirely
satisfactory moral outcome. In other cases, any one of several courses
of action might satisfy the standards. Typically, however, even in the
most difficult of cases, some solutions are in greater conformity with
these standards than others. Those solutions can be defended morally,
and police officers can come to reason through those defenses. Chapters
4 through 7 in this book illustrate the reasoning process by which the
five standards can be applied to morally significant policing situations.

We are well aware that officers do not have time in the heat of action
to develop carefully reasoned arguments on the relative merits of each
available option. Our aim is to provide for officers, students or general
readers a perspective from which they can think about what they would
do in certain recurring, difficult situations if they were to face them, or
to rethink what they have done if they have faced such a situation
before. Some officers prefer to think about stressful or difficult policing
issues in advance of facing them, and some police training is premised
on the fact that decision-making and action can be rehearsed. Those of
us who will not have to face these problems or decisions ourselves still
may wish to evaluate police behavior in light of developed standards
of behavior that officers should be expected to follow. Evaluation and
judgment take place in all of these contexts. As we noted earlier, police
work is now more open to public scrutiny than it was twenty-five years
ago. As a result, it is in the interests of both the police and the public
to make these judgments carefully and well. This book is our contribution to that process.

Most of what we have to say about the moral and ethical dimensions
of police work is drawn from our engagement with municipal police
officers performing uniformed patrol work. Since three-fourths of all
police resources are dedicated to uniformed patrol, this was a logical
focus for our training program and our development of police ethics
curriculum. We are less familiar with the moral and behavioral intri-
cacies of federal law enforcement, or long-term, deep-cover operations
such as ABSCAM. Thus, we have not addressed them systematically
in this book. Although we are hesitant to generalize about forms of
policing we have not studied as fully as municipal patrol work, our

standards are broad enough to encompass many forms of law enforcement.[4]

NOTES

1. Howard Cohen, "Working Ethics for Police Officers," *Criminal Justice Ethics* 1, no. 1 (Winter/Spring, 1982).

2. We offered IHLET seminars in Brunswick, Georgia; Baltimore, Maryland; Monmouth, Oregon; Albany, New York; and East Camden, Arkansas. We have also conducted seminars in Los Angeles, California; Reno, Nevada; and Waterville, Maine.

3. Howard Cohen and Michael Feldberg, *Ethics for Professional Policing* (Harvard, Mass.: Wasserman Associates, 1985).

4. Readers who wish to explore the moral issues associated with undercover police work in greater detail should consult the works of Gerald M. Caplan, Gary T. Marx, and Jerome Skolnick cited in the bibliography. We hope that our perspective on police ethics would illuminate and clarify the distinctive issues police face in those circumstances as well.

Part I

STANDARDS OF POLICE ETHICS

1

The Moral Dimensions of Police Work

Police work is especially interesting to the general public because it is a moral crucible in which the risks of the individual officer and the opportunities for moral action are magnified in relation to the more mundane lives of most people. Despite its moments of routine and boredom, policing throws its practitioners on a regular basis into extremely difficult and often complicated situations in which the officer has enormous potential to do harm or good. A police officer can turn a marital dispute into a family crisis, or the officer can help navigate the "beef" to the point where the feuding couple can reconcile. An officer called to the scene of a bar-room argument can prevent damage to persons and property, or become the flash point for an all-out brawl. An officer can, as a "professional courtesy," let a fellow officer drive home drunk, and either make a friend or create a tragedy—depending on whether the fellow officer makes it home safely or not. Arresting a teenager for a petty crime might turn out to be the best thing that ever happened to the youth, or the beginning of an unspeakable nightmare.

These and countless other decisions that police must make in the course of their work may have great impact on those of us on the receiving end of police services, and they certainly affect the moral character of the officers themselves. There is no sidestepping the moral dimensions of the job. Officers have to respond when they are dispatched. They are expected to intervene where there is conflict, social disruption or violation of the law. In responding, they are authorized by statute to be practitioners, in Egon Bittner's words, of "non-

negotiable force,'' that is, force that citizens are not permitted to resist.[1]
Officers are expected, with little time for contemplation, to act author-
itatively in situations where the resolution is not easily predicted. In
such situations, accountability for the outcome of events and choices
falls squarely on the individual officer. Police themselves are prone to
say, ''When you do something on this job, you wear it.'' Not acting
is also a form of moral decision-making that carries moral weight for
officers.

As society's peacekeepers and law enforcers, police have a considerable range of discretion to carry out their work. They are, of course,
not unrestricted free agents; there are laws and rules that govern police
conduct, and set limits to police authority and power. Departments have
policies that govern the ways police officers should conduct themselves
on the street. There are court-mandated procedures for interrogation
and arrest. Superior officers set priorities and guide the practices of
members of their squads. There are also the pressures of civil liabilities
and civil rights suits, and now, in an increasing number of departments,
accreditation standards.

However, for all of the efforts to regulate police work, there remains
broad opportunity for options and choices in performance of the job.
Jerome Skolnick[2] has shown that discretion extends to even the most
routine of police functions, ticketing a parking violation. Beyond the
routine aspects of the job, police work tends to be responsive to circumstances and to individuals within them. It is often up to the officer,
for example, to decide whether an arrestable offense has occurred and,
so, whether the procedures for arrest are to be followed. Officers can
see, or choose not to see, violations of the law. They can play up or
play down the significance of a situation and, as a result, make their
own involvement more or less formal. They can encourage the quick
resolution of a dispute, or they can send it into the legal system, leaving
it for court clerks, lawyers or judges to unravel.

Despite departmental and outside efforts to control and routinize
police behavior, police work remains essentially reactive, essentially
unsupervised at critical moments and essentially dependent upon the
judgment of the officer on the scene. We do not mean to ignore the
many areas of policing that are less confrontational. Some departments
have their officers spend considerable time on neighborhood problem-
solving and community relations. Nevertheless, there is an essential
core of police work that is grounded in authority and coercion, and it

is in those activities that the moral dimensions of the job become most clear and most significant. Policing can be a solitary job in which the officer makes decisions with little opportunity to discuss them with colleagues or supervisors before acting.

With discretion comes responsibility, and police officers are, by and large, held responsible for their own actions. There are, of course, differences among departments in their willingness to back up an officer against whom a complaint has been lodged. In some departments, an officer is presumed innocent until proven guilty; in others, the opposite assumption seems to hold. In general, patrol officers tend to protect one another and cover up each other's responsibility for mistakes and minor wrongdoing, lest they be blamed, disciplined or sued for their actions. Larger departments have created internal affairs units, whose role it is to investigate citizen complaints against officers as well as violations of department rules uncovered by supervisors. These units signal a department's intention to make each officer accountable for his or her own actions and decisions. William Ker Muir reports that the chief of the "Laconia" department that he studied was remorseless in his pursuit of officer wrongdoing. Departments of all sizes tend to hold officers accountable for living up to published rules and regulations, policies and procedures. Manuals covering these areas can be exceedingly complex and quite extensive. What departments do less well, if at all, is articulate and establish general moral standards against which officers' actions and decisions can be measured. In matters of morality, where written rules cannot provide guidance in decision-making, police officers stand pretty much on their own.[3]

From the moral point of view, police are not generally better equipped than the rest of us to make difficult and complicated moral decisions. Police are not recruited from the ranks of the saints, and they are not identified in youth and groomed in the moral virtues, as Plato suggested they ought to be in *The Republic*.[4] In general, American society does not channel people into future employment on the basis of temperament and moral character, and our society makes no effort to encourage any particular moral qualities in its police, though most of us would hope for honesty, courage and restraint.[5] Indeed, policing is a profession of middle-range status, one in which the market principles of selection probably operate pretty well. There are enough people who want to be police officers so that departments are able to be somewhat selective, and there is a large enough pool of jobs so that departments must select officers from a reasonably broad social spectrum. Police, by and large, tend to represent the moral values and outlook of the conventional, middle-class communities in which most of them reside. Skolnick, noting the pervasive influence of danger and authority in police work, locates them on the conservative end of the social spectrum.[6]

Because the main business of police work is enforcing the law and maintaining public order, it is important that the police, as the first line and most visible representation of government power, share a common outlook and what William Ker Muir, Jr. calls a "common sense"[7] with most of the rest of us. Although we might disagree with each other about who meets the definition of a moral paragon, it might be tempting to try to recruit police officers who were "morally superior" so that they would be less likely to become corrupt or lazy. As a democratic society, however, we would surely want to avoid creating such an elite corps of police and labeling its members "superior." We would not want them to feel authorized to think that their judgment about right and wrong, and good and bad would be superior to the rest of ours. Such a corps could easily become a threat to democracy. So, although we should be thankful that departments do not recruit and retain a class of officers who are regarded as morally superior to the rest of us, we must realize that this makes the work more difficult for them. Police tend to have no greater moral insight or powers of analysis than the rest of us, but they have jobs that throw them into more perilous situations. They are likely to experience a range of moral confrontation that is wider and more intense than most of us can expect—or would wish—to experience. This certainly makes police work interesting and instructive to us, and it helps us to see why it is useful to think of this job as a moral crucible.

In its most dramatic moments, police work can confront the question of whether to take human life. This responsibility is a rare occurrence in society generally, and not a common moral issue even for police. Some officers, however, will face it at some time in their careers, and all officers need to prepare for it. Contemporary police training usually takes up this question in video-training programs where the elements of justifiable shootings are analyzed in dramatic re-enactments of realistic situations. These programs can help trainees distinguish the legally justifiable from the unjustifiable uses of a firearm. That is, they help trainees know in which circumstances state law and departmental regulations permit them to fire their guns at someone. However, less frequently do such courses on the use of firearms confront the more subtle questions of whether, by taking more prudent or resourceful prior steps (waiting for backup, not confronting the suspect directly), the officer might have avoided getting into a position where he or she had to shoot at a suspect.

This issue reappears in any consideration of the use of coercive force—whether deadly or not. Officers are expected to use necessary force to accomplish their aims, but they are prohibited from using excessive force. The difference between what is necessary and what is excessive can sometimes depend upon how well an officer controlled a situation in its initial phases. To the extent that he or she let the situation get out of hand, the officer bears some responsibility for the harm or pain to suspects or members of the public that results from greater levels of coercion. Coercive force is permitted and even required in police work, and becomes a moral problem because its use is both permitted and limited.

The same might be said of the exercise of authority in general. Police have considerably more authority over others than most people in society and, consequently, have more opportunities to use that authority in impermissible ways. Police have opportunities, for example, to use their authority for personal gain. Many people are ready to offer gifts or favors to police officers in exchange for a "break," or for special consideration of one kind or another. That is not to say that officers are more likely to take advantage of these opportunities than others might, but only that they must regularly deal with the temptations. There is simply more moral pressure on police because their work brings them into contact with elements of crime and corruption from which others can steer clear.

Another dimension in which the moral pressures on police are greater than on other citizens is the demands of loyalty. Police work can drive its practitioners together in fraternal bonds that may invite the individual officer on occasion to compromise his or her personal standards of honesty and truthfulness. Few professionals place such a high premium on backing up fellow practitioners, virtually no matter what the circumstances.[8] Although officers strongly appreciate the importance of this "safety net" in the course of dangerous work, they are also uncomfortable when it is invoked as a shield for questionable acts. Most officers will maintain loyalty rather than report petty violations of department rules by a fellow officer. However, serious violations of criminal law are more likely to strain an officer's limits of loyalty. When discussing this topic, most officers say they would excuse the officer who sacrificed loyalty to colleagues if those colleagues were asking him to cover up their commission of a serious felony, such as selling hard drugs. Even one of the fiercest defenders of loyalty we ever met agreed he would draw the line at protecting a "killer cop." That being said, however, those same officers agree that the excused officer would risk paying a price for this act of disloyalty, such as being shunned by fellow officers. A well-known example is the story of Frank Serpico, who claimed he was shunned by fellow officers and did not receive backup on a drug raid because he would not go along with widespread departmental corruption.[9] This is a level of moral pressure or personal risk that few others must face in their professional lives.

Some police officers work in departments where covering up incompetence, brutality or corruption is part of the general atmosphere—what social scientists would call "structural immorality." These departments are debilitating to all officers who work in them, because they make policing with integrity impossible. Integrity is the virtue of approaching the world (in this case, one's work) from an undivided perspective that permits the officer to deal with others consistently and fairly. The "wholeness" that is implied by the concept of integrity is impossible if the officer must ignore special treatment for a favored few or mistreatment of a disfavored few. In such departments, wherever the individual officer looks, he or she can find few allies to stand up for integrity, lawful behavior or personal honesty. In some departments, the police are an extension of local politics, and the department's services are used to advance the political careers of elected officials, as dumping places for patronage appointees, or to reward elected officials' backers with the favor of non-enforcement of laws and ordinances (for example, allowing illegal parking in front of commercial businesses or restaurants and clubs owned by campaign contributors). Even those officers who will not go along with the illegalities compromise their sense of integrity by looking the other way rather than revealing these abuses. In sum, police officers may find themselves working in environments where the pressures toward cynicism and a loss of moral idealism are very great.

Were it not enough that police work puts its practitioners into morally difficult circumstances, it also puts them into circumstances where they are dealing with people in their most uncivil moments. People do not often "call the cops" to help celebrate happy occasions. The business of police work is to investigate crimes where people have been harmed in some way, to restore order where it has broken down and to aid those in need of help. These are some of the most stressful times in people's lives, and they are often thick with anger and pain. Often, people are not at their best when the police deal with them on a call. They may be irrational, incoherent, enraged, depressed or otherwise out of sorts. In short, they are anything but reasonable, polite and objective. Muir sizes up the typical police/citizen confrontation by noting: "The citizen is, relative to the policeman, the more dispossessed, the more detached, the nastier, and the crazier."[10] He goes on to say: "The policeman is the one who is on the defensive. . . . he demonstrates how difficult it is for the self-restrained person to defend himself against the bully."[11] In such circumstances, it is tempting for the officer to leave without doing much of anything helpful, or to use excessive force or make an arrest for the sake of terminating the incident.

What for most of us would be an unending series of moral watersheds, each a new opportunity for heroism or corruption, are for the police the normal and expected responsibilities of the job. To carry out these tasks, according to Skolnick, officers develop what he calls a "working personality."[12] This amounts to the pattern of attitudes and behaviors police adopt toward the people they encounter in their work. Officers must decide when to be tough and when to be compassionate, when to be strict and when to be flexible, when to compromise and when to draw a line that others cannot cross. In making these decisions and developing a style of policing, officers are also working out the difference between doing a favor and playing favorites, between necessary and excessive force, between public good and personal interest, and between enforcing laws and upholding the law.

In developing a working personality, the officer has room for choice. There is more than one way to do the job, although some ways are better than others. This is so both from the perspective of technical competence and the perspective of morality. Some officers adopt a style that is dominating and harsh; others can be quite conciliatory. Some sidestep complex issues; others wade into them with relish. These choices can make the work more or less difficult in specific situations; they also open the officer to moral judgment for better or for worse. Though there is a tendency in any profession to narrow the judgments of its practitioners to questions of technical competence, it is quite clear in police work that these questions carry moral significance as well. That is why police work is especially interesting to us, and why we can learn so much from exploring its moral dimensions.

THE SCHOLARLY RECOGNITION OF POLICING'S MORAL DIMENSION

Scholarly interest in the police as a subject of moral drama and moral illumination is comparatively recent. (Of course, literary interest in the police is of longer standing.) As we noted in the Introduction, the historic image of the American urban police has been associated with brutality and corruption rather than moral choice. When urban police forces developed in the nineteenth century, they fell under the control of state and local political machines, who used the police to protect vice and other activities that could be "shaken down" for funds to support the machines. As political agencies, police department allegiance was to the local ruling party, and in times of partisan conflict, officers could be quite repressive. What little interest there was in turning the police into moral agents was generated by blue-ribbon commissions who were usually trying to discredit an incumbent political machine. In the period prior to World War II, the idea of police ethics seemed to be something of a contradiction in terms, something "progressive reformers" and a few forward-looking police chiefs advocated but few other Americans demanded.[13]

The police community responded to politically motivated corruption inquiries and other prying under its moral rocks by "outsiders" with a closing of its ranks that made it difficult for outsiders to see what the police actually did. This periodic public scrutiny during blue-ribbon inquiries also led police apologists to propagate the "bad apple" theory of police immorality. That is, in response to documented cases of corruption and brutality, police administrators would declare them merely isolated deeds by "bad apple" officers. Bad apples were morally corrupt individuals, rotten on the inside and hiding under a skin of respectability, and who were only out for themselves. The vast majority of officers (the remainder of the barrel), we were assured, were morally upstanding and beyond temptation or excess. The rotten apples needed removal so that the barrel's other apples would not be contaminated; police administrators and apologists never conceded that the barrel might, itself, have been contaminated, much less that it might be the source of the problem.

As long as we are kept in the dark about the goings on in the apple barrel and assured that there are only a few bad ones in it, there is little about policing that is of moral interest. If officers are either saints or scoundrels, there is little we can learn from them. Police work is interesting for us to the extent that officers are in conflict about whether to do the right thing, or better yet, about what the right thing really is. It is these conflicts and their resolutions that can teach us something about morality.

It is only in the past twenty-five years or so that scholars have begun to penetrate the secrecy that supported the bad apple theory of police morality. The ground-breaking work was actually done in 1951 in a doctoral dissertation by William Westley. This work, however, was not published until 1970, when it appeared as *Violence and the Police*.[14] Westley's work, and others published from the mid–1960s through the late 1970s, brought to light a more accurate description of police work and an improved understanding of the moral dilemmas that it contains. This body of scholarly work has, in turn, permitted a more interesting artistic treatment of the police. The works of Joseph Wambaugh, the films *Serpico* and *Prince of the City*, and the television series "Hill Street Blues" depend upon our understanding that police are morally complex persons in morally taxing jobs. These works of "documentary fiction" contradict the bad apple theory, which reassures us that only a few cops are morally "bad" and that all the rest live up to some known ideal of the moral good.

The development of an accurate conception of police work and its moral ambiguities was hard won. Westley found the tendency of police officers to be secretive about their work a daunting barrier to understanding them or why they did what they did. Westley recounted a number of incidents involving questionable use of police tactics that slowed or interrupted his work because, not trusting Westley to cover them up, the police stopped talking to him. Nevertheless, as a result of his work and that of scholars who followed him, policing has become a better illuminated profession.

Westley began his study with a rejection of the bad apple conception of police morality. He assumed that in most departments, as in other organizations, individual behaviors and practices were shaped by organizational conflicts in attitudes and values.[15] Although departments that were thoroughly corrupt might have produced scoundrels, and departments that were thoroughly professional might have produced saints, most departments fell somewhere in between, producing officers whose behavior was sometimes questionable but capable of improvement. Westley believed that most officers were pretty ordinary people who found themselves in a particularly difficult line of work.[16] He wanted to understand how this work led its practitioners to sometimes commit acts of violence that he personally found quite abhorrent.

Westley saw the moral behavior of individual police officers as the product of general relations between police departments and the publics they serve. Based on his observation of one midwestern police department, Westley argued that police relations with the public were mutually hostile and distrustful.[17] This hostility isolates police departments from the public, which fosters values of silence, secrecy and solidarity among the officers, and in the department administration's dealings with the public and other segments of the criminal justice system.[18] These values, in Westley's view, create a police culture that tolerates, and even encourages, the use of violence against the public.

From Westley's sociological perspective, the way to address the moral problems of police violence is through changing the social structures that give rise to it. He makes a plea for better police/public relationships in order to reduce hostilities, and thereby weaken the need for police secrecy, silence and solidarity. When he published this work in 1970, twenty years after beginning it and in the midst of hostile race relations between urban blacks and municipal police departments, Westley added a postscript on the contemporary importance of improving these relations for preserving our democratic society.

Although the importance of Westley's work as a corrective to the bad apple theory is undeniable, it nevertheless had its deficiencies. Social scientists questioned both the validity and the reliability of his data. From our perspective, this work acknowledged, but did not yet capture, the moral complexity of police work. The focus on an external variable (public hostility) did not fully explain variations among individual officers' approaches to moral questions, nor did it sufficiently acknowledge each officer's responsibility in the decision-making process, that is, his or her use of discretion. Other scholars were to focus on these themes.

Jerome Skolnick, in his 1966 study *Justice Without Trial*,[19] drew on Westley's then unpublished dissertation but developed his own, more complex, analysis of police work. A major advance in Skolnick's study is his identification of structural conflicts within the job of policing that create moral dilemmas for all police officers. Skolnick observed that there was an inherent conflict between the two major roles of police in a democracy: maintaining order and upholding the rule of law.[20] Law is both an instrument of order and its adversary.[21]

Police must use the law to maintain order, but the law also protects the rights of the suspect, sometimes at the expense of efficiency. Police work, in Skolnick's analysis, is grounded in the elements of danger, authority and efficiency. In the context of these elements, officers tend to feel isolated from the public and suspicious of the people they deal with.[22] Skolnick shares with Westley the view that police are fairly conventional people in their own moral outlook who must deal with unconventional, and sometimes immoral, characters.[23] Possessing the authority to keep order, officers must also limit their behavior to actions permitted by law and the Constitution. Even when feeling endangered by the potential violence of others, police must use only minimal necessary force to protect themselves. Unlike Westley, Skolnick sees the conflict that these contradictory circumstances create as deeply embedded within police work itself. That is, it is not just external relations with the public that creates the moral conflict within the officer; it is the need both to maintain order through coercive force, on the one hand, and, on the other, to respect the rule of law, individual rights and the limits of government authority.

Skolnick took his analysis of the moral circumstances of the police beyond Westley's account in other ways as well. First, he recognized that the moral issues of police work extended well beyond brutality and corruption. Skolnick saw that virtually every activity that the police undertook had the potential to create harm or benefit for citizens. As he acknowledged in his title, police work is about justice—as it is dispensed on the street as well as in the courtroom. Seen in this light, even the issuing (or not issuing) of a parking citation can become a moral question. Is the officer being even-handed? Should he recognize extenuating circumstances? Should she give someone a break if it is deserved? Skolnick reviews a wide variety of police activities to demonstrate that they all involve significant questions of justice.

A second important development in Skolnick's analysis is its emphasis on officer discretion. Even in the most routine matters, officers have choices to make, and they make them. An officer about to write a citation on an expired meter may decide not to, if the driver returns with change. A public disturbance may end with an arrest or a command to clear the street. A prostitute may be arrested or left to be taken in another time. These decisions are the officer's to make. In most cases there is not strict department policy about how to handle matters of peacekeeping and public order. Discretion is given to officers—they have not merely usurped it. Morally, this means that the police legitimately may make judgments in dispensing justice. Their moral dilemmas are not merely covert or de facto; they are designed into the job. This means that police morality is not an underground morality: it is an important part of the work and deserving of public scrutiny.

A third scholar who advanced our understanding of the moral dilemmas of police work is Jonathan Rubinstein. In his 1973 study, *City Police*,[24] Rubinstein undertakes a careful and detailed description of police work. As he says in his preface, "Before any judgment of its moral character or suggestions for reforming it can be made, the work itself must be described."[25] A journalist by profession, Rubinstein's description of policing is based on his personal experience of academy training and street duty in Philadelphia between 1969 and 1971. Rubinstein's account of the characteristics of policing is thus constructed from the practitioner's perspective, and is as thorough a description as any we have of the duties and priorities of police work as it actually occurs, rather than as it might appear in an official job description. Rubinstein's work is particularly sensitive to what has come to be called "police culture." He describes police work not merely as a set of tasks, but as an officer's style of working and his systematic orientation toward the people he polices and toward his fellow officers.

Rubinstein's contribution to our understanding of the moral circumstances of police work is, first, that he was able to document the way officers define and accept responsibility for the consequences of their own actions. Rubinstein describes how officers draw a distinction between crimes and disturbances that take place in public spaces within their jurisdiction ("outside" acts) and crimes and disturbances that take place in areas where they are not reasonably expected to know about them ("inside" acts). Inside acts, such as marital rape, child abuse or even a burglary that occurred when the thief cut a hole in the roof of a commercial establishment, cannot be seen as the officer's professional responsibility because he or she could not have prevented or detected them; outside acts, such as muggings or gang fights, no matter how unpreventable, reflect on the officer's competence and control of his or her beat. Officers treat outside acts very seriously,[26] and accept the idea that an officer is to be judged professionally in relation to his or her ability to deal with outside acts.

Rubinstein also addressed the question raised by both Westley and Skolnick concerning the extent to which officers' moral behavior is shaped by the structure and culture of the job. Skolnick described an inherent conflict between the demands of maintaining order and the demands of upholding the due process of law. Rubinstein takes this insight further and identifies specific dilemmas for officers who want to act professionally, for example, both to keep order and uphold the rule of law. Focusing particularly on vice work, Rubinstein observes:

> Many of the illegal things that policemen do are not designed to generate payoffs for them but to meet obligations established by the department. If the patrolman were freed from having to make vice arrests, only the corrupt, the money-hungry, would continue to do the illegal things so many policemen do. There are no *legal* ways to enforce the drug laws on the streets, so any pressure on the police to make more drug arrests is an open encouragement to them to lie and violate their pledge to uphold the Constitution.[27] (emphasis added)

The moral problem here is not that police officers are faced with a choice between right and wrong where doing the wrong thing is a great temptation. Rather, it is that they are faced with a choice between doing one or another "right" thing—each of which undermines the other. As Rubinstein saw it, in order to control the use and sale of drugs officers had to violate the rights of addicts and dealers. In order to respect the rights of all citizens (addicts and dealers included), officers must be resigned to their failure to control drug use—even though they know society wants them to do "something" about drugs. The moral complexity of this problem is apparent, and the resolution is bound to be at least partly unsatisfactory.

Of course not all police work is vice work—or even very much like vice work in the clarity of the dilemmas it poses. Nevertheless, the moral problems Rubinstein illuminates are real and far from rare in police work. Officers experience these problems and, if they face them often enough without finding some resolution to them, the officers can develop cynicism about the possibility of doing their job "correctly," that is, resolving the competing claims of maintaining order on their beats without violating individual rights and the due process of law. As we recognize this complexity, it becomes clear that the moral dimensions of police work are worthy of much more attention, both within and outside departments.

Herman Goldstein, in his 1977 work, *Policing a Free Society*,[28] argues that police administrators must openly acknowledge the range and magnitude of their officers' discretion, and take steps to guide and supervise its use. After describing the breadth of the police function and the need for police to have an expanded set of tools (beyond arrest) to deal with the social-service functions of police work, Goldstein makes a plea for "formalizing the informal"[29] (i.e., structuring discretion). He categorizes the kinds of situations in which police exercise discretion with an eye toward identifying those that should be recognized and supervised by the command staff. Referring to the work on discretion by Kenneth Culp Davis, Goldstein argues that discretion not be eliminated, but rather that it be "structured."[30] He believes that the quality of police service will be improved if the proper use of discretion is acknowledged and taught.[31]

The importance of Goldstein's work from the perspective of police ethics is that he moved the debate from the classroom and the locker room to the administrative offices of police departments. If police administrators must acknowledge that their officers exercise discretion extensively during the course of doing their jobs, then those administrators must take some responsibility for helping their officers make the right decisions. Goldstein put the conclusions of sociologists into language that chiefs and captains could understand.

The social scientist who made the most progress in clarifying the moral dimensions of police choice-making from the perspective of the individual officer was William Ker Muir, Jr., who published his work, *Police: Streetcorner Politicians*, in 1977.[32] Muir's most important contribution to our understanding of the moral dimension of police work is his demonstration that individual officers, while working within the same department's "culture," still manage to respond to the core moral dilemmas of policing in a variety of ways, some of which are better than others. Prior to his work, scholars tended to treat police behavior as relatively homogeneous. They either described police practices that conformed to a police culture, or they described the dominant or typical police response to a standard moral problem that officers might face. This approach tended to illuminate individual moral actions as products of the social structure of policing rather than as products of the decisions made by individual officers. Muir makes it clear that, within the structure of police work, the officer still can choose among a variety of responses. It is the development of different response patterns in different officers, that is to say their characters, that interests Muir.[33]

Muir begins with the question: Does power corrupt?[34] By this, Muir asks whether officers can use coercive force to do their assigned work without falling into illegal, brutal, cynical or indifferent patterns of behavior—the various attitudes and behavior so well documented by Rubinstein. Unlike Rubinstein, Muir does not characterize police work as a series of insoluble dilemmas. Rather, he sees the most important police/citizen relationships as what he calls "extortionate transactions"[35] in which police have official authority, but citizens, paradoxically, can acquire the upper hand by virtue of their relative dispossession, detachment, remorselessness or irrationality when compared to the officer who is confronting them. Under these conditions, the officer's task is to find a style of policing that will permit him or her to use coercive force effectively against the irrational or otherwise out-of-control citizen, without going beyond the limits of law in controlling or coercing that individual and without losing interest in the humanity of the individual being policed.

In his research, Muir identifies four styles of policing, each of which represents the way in which officers tend to respond to extortionate transactions with citizens. These four styles Muir calls the professional, the reciprocator, the enforcer and the avoider.[36] Under the pressures of dealing with dispossessed, detached, remorseless and irrational citizens, officers tended to develop in one or another of these directions, and those who developed in the direction of the professional were, on the whole, the best officers in Muir's view. These four styles are the product of an officer's attitudes on two key matters of moral value: (1) the officer's outlook on human nature as he or she encountered it in the course of policing people, and (2) the officer's ability to integrate the use of necessary force in police work into his or her outlook on life.[37]

According to Muir's classification, officers who see human nature in dualistic terms ("us vs. them," the "honest people vs. the crooks" or "new centurions vs. the barbarians") and who feel conflicted about the use of force tend to be avoiders. These officers do not see most people in poor or "bad" neighborhoods as worth defending, and they lack the assertiveness to be comfortable exercising their authority against intim-

idating characters with whom they are unfamiliar. They thus leave the
"good" people in these neighborhoods defenseless against those of
their neighbors and family members who act as criminal predators and
intimidators. Officers who see human nature in dualistic terms but who
are confident of the propriety of the use of force, tend to be enforcers.
Officers who see human nature in more unitary terms ("we are all cut
from the same human cloth, even when some of us commit crimes or
disturb the peace") but who are conflicted about the use of force, tend
to be reciprocators. This type of officer will bargain with those he or
she seeks to control rather than demand their compliance with his or
her orders. Officers who see human nature in unitary terms and who
are comfortable with the use of force to achieve the legitimate ends of
police work Muir calls professionals (that is, they are firm but compassionate in their exercise of authority).

For Muir, adopting a style of policing is a moral choice—professionals are the best officers, and not simply in a technical sense. The
officer's training academy, supervising sergeant and department chief
can all have influence, but the choice to act morally is finally made by
each individual officer. All four styles are possible in most departments,
and officers who develop into professionals will be able to do their
work well and resist corruption in its broadest sense; that is, to resist
the opportunity to overuse or underuse their authority.

Muir's work has made it possible to shift the perspective on police
ethics from social science to moral philosophy. Although Muir is himself
a social scientist, his work does not treat police behavior as little more
than an artifact of the structural conditions of police work. He has
demonstrated that, within the context of that work, there is room for
choice, and that the available choices are based on individual attitudes
and outlooks that have to do with an officer's fundamental moral values
regarding human nature and the use of force.

The works described above, and the works of other scholars writing
since the 1960s, have made it possible to investigate police behavior
as an area of applied ethics. The work of sociologists laid the groundwork, by the end of the 1970s and beginning of the 1980s, for philosophers to bring general moral analysis to bear on the structural problems
of police work. In the way that sociologists are specialists in describing
group behavior and identifying patterns in it, philosophers are specialists
in discussing morality and the ethical standards against which human

conduct can or should be judged. Philosophers can offer a moral perspective from which to examine the canvas of human experience.

One recent approach to the moral problems of policing develops the role of character in confronting the moral pressures inherent in this occupation. Edwin J. Delattre's *Character and Cops* argues that the police mission and public reliance on, or trust in, the police as a social force demand a certain excellence of character.[38] Departments, in his view, should recruit or develop individuals who are not only self-controlled, but who also take pride in their own virtue.[39] The virtues required of a police officer include trustworthiness, temperate judgment, incorruptability, courage and competence. In Delattre's view, the moral difficulties in police work have less to do with knowing what is the right thing to do than with having the fortitude to do it in the face of pressures to act otherwise. In his discussion of Character and Free Will, Delattre makes it clear that the honorable path is not always easy to follow, but that the responsibility to do so resides squarely with the officer.[40] As he puts it in another context: "Those who have no stomach for such ordeals of the public trust should find another line of work."[41]

Delattre believes that police work demands a "higher standard" of its practitioners.[42] If they meet that standard, they will be above the temptations of immorality. His message is that police can meet that standard, and that many officers have done so. A substantial portion of his work is devoted to describing instances of police work of high quality performed by officers of excellent character.

Delattre reminds us that many situations are not morally ambiguous, even when they are difficult. Theft, extortion and brutality are wrong, and one does not need a refined moral sense to know this. Nevertheless, there are circumstances that police encounter that are genuinely ambiguous, circumstances where it is not easy to know what is the right thing to do. Delattre's approach offers limited guidance to the officer in such "grey areas." Our own approach differs from Delattre's in that we particularly focus on the ways in which the moral standards that govern police work can guide behavior in those ambiguous situations—the "grey areas"—that seem to arise so often in the course of policing. Even officers who are not exemplars of virtue day in and day out are expected to make the effort to do the right thing, and need guidance in this effort, a clear understanding of how their choices will be evaluated and instruction in ways to choose better the next time around. In our approach to police ethics, we are attempting to clarify both the standards of evaluation and the reasoning process through which they are applied to ambiguous cases. The perspective described in the next chapter offers a vantage point from which to see police behavior in the broader context of American political values and the ideals that form the basis of our current political institutions.

NOTES

1. Technically, citizens can resist "excessive" police force, but the meaning of excessive is usually determined after an incident is finished and the aggrieved citizen files a complaint to initiate legal action against the officer who allegedly employed the excessive force.

2. Jerome H. Skolnick, *Justice Without Trial* (New York: John Wiley, 1966), ch. 4.

3. There is, of course, a departmental culture that creates expectations about how things are to be done in the absence of rules and regulations. Although that culture may help officers to know how their fellow officers will view their behavior, it cannot assure an officer that the department command staff will either alter its judgment of officer behavior or deflect responsibility for the officer's action. Nor does it assure that the cultural norm of the department is morally sound.

4. Plato, *The Republic* (Baltimore: Penguin Books, 1955).

5. A more recent investigation of the relationship between police work and a police officer's moral character is Edwin J. Delattre's *Character and Cops* (Washington, D.C.: American Enterprise Institute for Public Policy Research, 1989).

6. Skolnick, *Justice Without Trial*, p. 59.

7. William Ker Muir, Jr., *Police: Streetcorner Politicians* (Chicago: University of Chicago Press, 1977), p. 35.

8. Doctors have some reputation for backing up other doctors in questions of medical malpractice, but it is unlikely that many doctors would refuse to give a second opinion for fear of contradicting a fellow practitioner.

9. Peter Maas, *Serpico* (New York: Viking Press, 1973).

10. Muir, *Police: Streetcorner Politicians*, p. 45.

11. Ibid.

12. Skolnick, *Justice Without Trial*, ch. 4.

13. Robert Fogelson, *Big-City Police* (Cambridge, Mass.: Harvard University Press, 1977).

14. William A. Westley, *Violence and the Police* (Cambridge, Mass.: MIT Press, 1970).

15. Ibid., p. xii.

16. Ibid., p. 47.

17. Ibid., p. 107.

18. Ibid., pp. 110–18.

19. Skolnick, *Justice Without Trial*, p. 45.

20. Ibid., p. 6.

21. Ibid., p. 7.

22. Ibid., pp. 42–44.

23. Ibid., pp. 56–61.

24. Jonathan Rubinstein, *City Police*, (New York: Ballantine Books, 1973).

25. Ibid., p. x.

26. Ibid., p. 341.

27. Ibid., p. 377.

28. Herman Goldstein, *Policing a Free Society* (Cambridge, Mass.: Ballinger, 1977).

29. Ibid., p. 82.

30. Ibid., p. 109.

31. Ibid., p. 110.

32. William Ker Muir, Jr., *Police: Streetcorner Politicians*.

33. See also Edwin J. Delattre, *Character and Cops* (Washington, D.C.: American Enterprise Institute for Public Policy Research, 1989).

34. Muir, *Police: Streetcorner Politicians*, p. 4.

35. Ibid., pp. 37–46.

36. Ibid., p. 145.

37. Ibid.

38. Delattre, *Character and Cops*, pp. 8–15.

39. Ibid., p. 9.

40. Ibid., pp. 82–86.

41. Ibid., p. 64.

42. Ibid., p. 68.

2

A Social Contract Perspective on the Police Role

Police ethics, like all professional ethics, must be grounded in a broader moral perspective. A moral perspective is a point of view that highlights the moral and ethical dimensions of actions and events. The perspective helps us examine human actions in a moral light, so that we can make value judgments about what is good or bad, or what is right or wrong. From a moral perspective, the field of police ethics particularly has some clear rights and wrongs. For example, refusing a bribe is not only following department rules or the dictates of law but is doing the right and honorable thing. Except for the special case in which a police officer was acting as part of an anti-corruption investigation, there is no moral perspective that could justify taking a bribe.

Most of the time, our judgments do not require a very refined moral perspective. Each of us has a notion of common decency that is widely accepted in our society. We have learned it from our parents and our teachers. It is incorporated into religious teachings and espoused by national leaders. We pick it up from observation, experience and instruction. This is not to say that what we have learned is a carefully articulated moral theory, but "common decency" does provide a shared sense of right and wrong. Most of us believe that it is wrong to steal, to cheat at cards or to do violence to innocent children. It is right to keep your promises, to help people in need and be fair in your dealings with others.

Common decency can take most of us a long way as we deal with life's difficulties or deal with other people. However, when we think of making moral judgments about police, we quickly realize that we cannot easily comprehend their actions or their moral situation in terms of common decency alone. Police have more power than the average citizen and are authorized to use force where others are forbidden. They are expected to keep social order, even when the rest of us have the impulse to carouse, to protest or even to riot. Finally, they are expected to operate in dangerous circumstances, risking their safety so we can have ours. Their duties and their working environment often place the police in situations where common decency has broken down. Holding them to its standards can be irrelevant or worse in extreme circumstances, such as negotiating with hostage-takers. It is often inappropriate to judge police work by the standards we would use for common social interaction or even business dealings.

Our assumption is that we need a different, more appropriate moral perspective for evaluating police work. It is important to remember that police work is a public function; that is, a political and governmental function. Police work is a form of public service, much as fire-fighting, emergency medical care or primary education are public services. In modern society, providing police service is a fundamental duty of government. Seen in this light, the moral basis of police work can be found in the moral basis of government activity itself.

A BRIEF HISTORY OF SOCIAL CONTRACT THEORY

Social contract theory provides an appropriate moral foundation for understanding and evaluating police practices. The theory lies at the very foundation of our society's social arrangements and its form of government. The nation's most important political documents, the Declaration of Independence and the Constitution, deeply reflect the influence of seventeenth- and eighteenth-century social contract philosophy. Thomas Jefferson, chief drafter of the Declaration, was a careful student of the English political theorists Thomas Hobbes and John Locke, leading articulators of social contract theory. It seems appropriate, therefore, that our theory of police ethics should be grounded in a broader political theory that has shaped the structure and practice of American government. After all, the police are among the most visible agents of government and, for most of us, agents of government that are highly identifiable on the street.

This contractual perspective on the police is especially helpful because it is the perspective that underlies our own form of government—a perspective articulated in the Declaration of Independence and the Constitution. As noted previously, the idea of the social contract, as it has come into our own political history, was articulated most clearly by two seventeenth-century English political writers, Thomas Hobbes and John Locke. Caught up in two separate seventeenth-century revolutions in which English monarchies were being challenged and even overthrown, these two men asked the question, "What is the basis of political authority?" With some variation, Hobbes and Locke each developed the image of government as the outcome of an agreement among citizens. More precisely, the theory of the social contract treats *both government itself and the authority it exercises* as the products of a bargain or compact struck between rulers and citizens. That bargain identifies the rights and obligations of each party to the relationship.

Although the social contract perspective is deeply ingrained in American political culture, we have not, of course, taken it over from seventeenth-century England without change. It is important to remember that both Hobbes and Locke thought of society as a society of property holders. They did not include in their thinking about political rights and political participation women, the poor or those in bondage. Social contract theory does not speak to issues of democracy or universal suffrage. It addresses, rather, issues about the sources and limits of governmental authority.

Thomas Hobbes argued that political authority derived from the presumed consent of the governed rather than from a divine right bestowed by God on a hereditary monarch. Hobbes made this argument in his best-known work, *Leviathan* (1649),[1] as England was headed for civil war over a struggle between Charles I, who claimed to rule by divine right, and Parliament, which tried to subject Charles to its laws. Eventually, Parliament won out and ordered Charles beheaded. Oliver Cromwell, at the invitation of Parliament, assumed political authority as the head of state. Cromwell's authority could not be grounded in the divine right of a king—he had no blood connection to a hereditary monarch—but Hobbes defended Cromwell's authority by arguing that it rested in the *office* of the ruler rather than his *personhood*.[2]

Political authority, as Hobbes conceived it, was given over by each person in society, unanimously and collectively, to an individual or individuals who could protect them from each other and protect them from a life that would otherwise inevitably be "solitary, poor, nasty, brutish and short."[3] In exchange for taking on the obligation to protect the lives of citizens and to create the secure conditions that would permit a reasonable life for each of them, citizens grant the ruler authority to make laws and the power needed to enforce them. During the revolutionary years of the 1640s, the terms in which Hobbes described the origins of government authority (improved chances for citizens' lives and security in exchange for their grant of authority and power to the ruler) must have seemed a reasonable bargain—at least to property holders. Nevertheless, one criticism that has since been applied to Hobbes's ideas is that they imposed few limits on the behavior or power of the ruler. So long as he provided security for the lives and property of citizens, he could choose virtually any of the means by which he governed.

John Locke was also writing about these issues in another revolutionary era, although the "Glorious Revolution" of 1688 was hardly as perilous as the civil war forty years earlier. In 1660, after the Cromwell years, Parliament restored the Stuarts to the English throne: Charles II, son of the beheaded former king, ruled until his own death in 1685; his brother, James II, succeeded him. The restoration of the Stuart monarchy in effect reopened the question of whether kings ruled by divine right or by consent of the governed. All of the issues between king and Parliament that had been contested in the 1640s were contested again. Supporters of the king published vigorous defenses of divine right theory. A friend of the parliamentary party, Locke penned his *First Treatise on Civil Government* (1688),[4] which systematically attacked the writings of divine right apologist Robert Filmer. Locke's better-known *Second Treatise*[5], published in 1691, was dedicated to the reign of William and Mary of Orange, who Parliament invited to England from the Netherlands in 1685 to replace the exiled James II. Once again, Parliament's forcible removal of a monarch needed justification and, like Hobbes, Locke did this through a theory of political legitimacy based on the notion of consent of the governed.

In the *Second Treatise*, Locke identified the purpose of government as providing safety and security to the governed, and he attempted to demonstrate why any reasonable person would accept these services from government rather than trying to provide them for himself or herself. Locke's version of the social contract establishes a more limited form of government than that envisioned by Hobbes. No doubt conditions in England in Locke's time were less severe, and a rational person would be less inclined to give so much power to an authority when the alternative was not so dire. The American Founding Fathers were deeply influenced by Locke's concept of a limited government, based on a social contract, and grounded in the consent of the governed. They found in the *Second Treatise* both the justification for separation from England in 1776 and the blueprint for a federal form of national government in 1787.

The Declaration of Independence asserts, in effect, that the government of England was no longer keeping its bargain with the citizens of the American colonies. The Declaration begins with Locke's assertion that "all men are created equal" and that they have rightful claims to life, liberty and property (Jefferson substituted "happiness" for "property" in the Declaration).[6] In Locke's view, the rights are inalienable, that is, cannot be either taken or even given away, because they are not granted by government (people would have them even in a "State of Nature," that is, a condition in which government did not exist). Nor, even after government is formed, are the individual's rights simply surrendered completely to that government. The purpose of government as the American Founding Fathers described it is simply to "secure" those rights that citizens already possess but have difficulty maintaining on their own. This is why people consent to give over or transfer their own authority to government—why they choose to become part of society rather than spend all their energies in the struggles of self-defense and defense of their material goods. Government, in a sense, is the agent of the citizens, providing collective security more effectively than sovereign individuals could do for themselves.

The Founding Fathers took from Locke the idea that, when a government no longer protects the individual's rights to life, liberty and property, it breaks its contract with the citizenry. In turn, citizens have a right, even a duty, to replace that government with another that will do a more effective job of providing for "safety and happiness." In a few short paragraphs, the authors of the Declaration presented the outlines of Locke's account of governmental authority before going on to list in detail the ways in which they felt the English government had abused or undermined it.

Locke's influence extended to the creation of the Constitution as well. The Constitution bears Locke's stamp in the sense that it structures the federal government along the lines of the three main governmental functions outlined in the *Second Treatise*: legislative, executive and judicial.[7] The Constitution goes beyond Locke's thinking in that it separates these functions into different branches of government, and places them in a system of checks and balances. Locke was not troubled by the possibility of joining all three functions into a single office or constitutional monarch, but the American experience under the reign of King George III would have made such an arrangement unthinkable by 1787, when the Constitution was drafted.

The Lockean underpinnings of the Constitution are also apparent in the general line of defense of the Constitution that appeared in the *Federalist Papers*, a series of newspaper editorials written by Alexander Hamilton, James Madison and John Jay meant to encourage electors in the various states to adopt the proposed Constitution of 1787, rather than continue American government under the Articles of Confederation.[8] The Federalist argument in favor of the Constitution begins from the problem of security in a hostile world, in effect, the problem of life in the state of nature (that is, life without government). In *Federalist Paper* No. 15, Hamilton stressed the importance of "safety and happiness" for society, and argued that both were threatened by the "anarchy" that he saw emerging under the weak form of national government authorized under the Articles of Confederation.[9] By creating a stronger central government, the Constitution promised to become the new social compact that would free the United States from that anarchy. The Federalists urged its adoption on the grounds that it provided the judicious balance of "stability and energy of government" on the one side, with liberty and representation on the other (*Federalist* No. 37).[10]

THE POLICE AND SOCIAL CONTRACT THEORY

Although both Locke and the Founding Fathers speak of government in general rather than police in particular, the social contract perspective permits a more detailed account of the powers and obligations of specific government agents. It is possible, from the perspective of the social contract, to explain the difference between the proper exercise of police authority (such as arresting a person who is the subject of a warrant) and the abuse of police authority (demanding cash from local tavern owners not to check the I.D.s of their young-looking patrons), between equal protection of citizens (not picking out black teenagers for harassment) and special privileges for some citizens (letting a personal friend or relative walk away from a drunk-driving offense), and between protecting citizens' liberty and security (proactive patrolling of high-crime areas) and jeopardizing the safety and security of the citizenry (conducting a high-speed auto chase on a busy city street).

It is worth looking a little more closely at John Locke's understanding of the social contract in order to see exactly how the responsibilities and obligations of public officials, particularly the police, can be derived from this perspective. Most of the interest by political theorists in the social contract has focused on questions of the source of sovereign authority in the people, the responsibilities of the citizenry to obey authority and the limits of authority in circumstances of revolutionary change. Less discussed, but of primary importance here, is the question of the obligations of those in authority to the citizenry. Locke, as we noted earlier, developed his conception of political authority in contrast to the idea of authority enunciated by the kings and queens of Europe, who claimed they inherited their thrones from God's biblical grant of the earth to Adam and his descendants. Similarly, Locke rejected the idea that political authority was that of "a father over his children, a master over his servant, a husband over his wife [or] a lord over his slave."[11] Rather, political authority is its own kind of power relationship. As Locke wrote:

Political power I take to be a right of making laws with penalties of death, and consequently all less[er] penalties, for the regulating and preserving [of] property, and of employing the force of the community, in execution of such laws, and in defense of the commonwealth from foreign injury; and all this only for the public good.[12]

To explain the extent and limits of this right of the "political power" to make and enforce laws, Locke introduced the concept of the State of Nature.[13] As we have noted, the State of Nature is Locke's name for the idea of human society without civil government—without a political authority. Locke asks us to consider what life would be like in a situation in which every person has freedom (everyone makes their own decisions) and equality (no one has authority over anyone else).[14] In such a condition, he suggests, people would live their lives without common authority: no law, no rules and no regulations. In our time, this would mean no taxes and no municipal services, such as public schools, libraries, fire departments and police. Each person would be free from the authority of others; there would be no public officials to compel us to drive on the right side of the road (if there were roads). Conversely, there would be no city hospital to go to if we were hurt, no police to call if our property were stolen, or no army to summon if our land were invaded. Each would be responsible for his or her survival and protection. In a State of Nature, in other words, we would each be on our own.

In such a State of Nature, individuals would have *liberty*.[15] For Locke, liberty means both freedom from restraints imposed by others (nobody has the right to stop you from doing what you want as long as you are not interfering with anyone else's rights), and freedom to decide what you want to do or be and pursue it.[16] In Locke's State of Nature, each person has the liberty to create a life and acquire property as he or she sees fit. No government official can confiscate that property through taxation or by eminent domain simply by claiming that it is needed for the common good. In other words, private property is strictly private, and no one else can have a claim on it.

Although it is true that each individual is free from the authority of others in the State of Nature, there are still some limits on how we ought to behave. Locke expressed this by saying that, even in a State of Nature, we are each subject to the "Law of Nature."[17] The Law of Nature, which we can know through our capacity to reason, tells us that "no one ought to harm another in his life, health, liberty or possessions."[18] Everyone is bound to "preserve himself" and, "as much as he can, preserve the rest of mankind." This law is not a creation of legislatures but something inherent in Nature, and so applies to people even where there are no governments or, even where governments do exist, no common jurisdiction.

Because Nature has its own law, people who are "harmed" by others have recourse. Everyone has the right to enforce the Law of Nature. That is, in a State of Nature, each individual also has the right of self-protection and the right to enforce his or her own rights.[19] If someone takes my property, I have the right to take it back and to impose a penalty on the person who took it. I do not have to obtain a warrant from a court to search for my missing goods, and I need not wait for a police officer to conduct the investigation. Nor do I need a court to tell me what penalty to impose on the individual who stole my goods, should I find that person (or decide that I probably found him or her).

After all, in a State of Nature, where there is no common authority (government), institutions such as courts and the police do not exist. The State of Nature is not particularly likely to be a tranquil, co-operative society. Although it is possible that people without a common authority might live peacefully, it is also possible, indeed likely, that some people will attempt to take advantage of the physical weakness of others. The strong would try to steal property from and even enslave the weak. In those circumstances, the State of Nature simply becomes a state of war[20] (Hobbes called it the "war of all against all"). The threat of war highlights the greatest deficiency of the State of Nature: individuals in it lack security.[21]

In the State of Nature, there is no one in authority to help me enforce my rights, protect my property and maintain my liberty. If others more powerful than I decide to interfere with my liberty or take my property, how can I stop them? There is no authority I can call on for help—no sheriff to ride into town at high noon and shoot the "bad guys" for me. I have the right to retaliate against them, of course, but since my tormentors are more powerful than I, how can I exercise this right? I could get a gun, an "equalizer," but so could my tormentors. Self-defense is not effective here. In a State of Nature, I would always be looking over my shoulder, watching out to see that no one was threatening my property or encroaching on my liberty. I would be preoccupied with self-protection. Each time I accumulated anything of value, I would feel like an exposed target. As soon as my life became a little more comfortable, it would also become a little more insecure.

Since a life like this would be intolerable, reasonable people would look for a better way to live together. In Locke's words:

Men being . . . by nature all free, equal and independent, no one can be put out of his estate and subjected to the political power of another without his own consent, which is done by agreeing with other men, to join and unite in a community for their comfortable, safe and peaceable living, one amongst another, in secure enjoyment of their properties, and a greater security than any that are not of it.[22]

Free, rational people see the advantages of a more secure life and therefore would voluntarily choose to leave the State of Nature for life in an organized community, that is, political (civil) society. Locke calls the process by which individuals make the choice to live in political society a "compact,"[23] or social contract. In every bargain or contract, individuals exchange something they have and are willing to part with for something they want but lack. In a State of Nature, people have liberty and lack security. Reasonable people would trade some of their liberty for increased security.

As we noted earlier, the liberty that individuals have in a State of Nature includes the liberty to enforce their own rights. That is, they have the freedom to protect themselves and their property from threats by others. Of course, for the relatively weak, these rights are difficult to enforce; even for the strong, it is almost impossible to protect oneself all the time, or to fight off coalitions of others who outweigh or out-number even the strongest individual.

Since in a bargain one gives up something he already has in order to get something he does not, under the social contract each individual transfers to an authority the liberty to enforce his own rights (not much of a sacrifice) in exchange for greater security (an indisputable benefit). The contract is the means by which individuals designate an agent (the state or government) to act on their behalf. This agent exercises the individuals' rights to safety and security by making rules for common living (for example, that no one may take the property of another without due process of law; no person may kill another except in self-defense; no one may enter the home of another uninvited). The end result is a trade-off: although individuals in civil society may have less liberty to pursue their private ends, they have greater security to enjoy the fruits of their labor. Their agent, government, has assumed the burden of protecting their lives, their property and their remaining liberty to de-velop their lives as they see fit.

Because Locke thinks of the social contract as a bargain, he insists that each individual who is a party to it should be thought of as having consented to it.[24] It is consent that binds individuals to the decisions made and actions taken by political authorities.[25] This consent may be explicit or tacit.[26] Tacit consent is given by those who "enjoy" or benefit from the laws of a political society. Locke regards mere benefit as a reasonable sign of consent, because he thinks it would be a con-tradiction to accept society's protection but deny the grounds on which it rests.[27] In other words, everyone is a party to the social contract, without exception, even if some refuse to recognize this condition. Given Locke's focus on property holders, we can understand the force of the tacit consent argument. Surely the benefits of protection of property are considerable in most societies. The argument is less compelling for the dispossessed. It is not so clear that a rational person with nothing—and nothing to lose—would agree to civil society over the State of Nature. Having noted this point, though, it is also worth remembering that the obligations of those in authority to "citizens" and "aliens" alike are not diminished by their inclusion in or exclusion from the social contract. All fall under the jurisdiction of the common authority.

Locke's conception of consent of the governed helps to clarify another point: the social contract is not a historical document.[28] To be sure, Locke thinks there may have been times in history when free people did come together and agree to create a government.[29] However, his point is that each rational person voluntarily consents to the necessary existence of political authority. The social contract—the deal struck among all those who comprise society—is only a hypothetical bargain. We do not actually sign a contract when we are born or when we become old enough to vote. Rather, we live together *as if* we had. When we contemplate the advantages and disadvantages of the State of Nature compared to civil society, we as rational individuals would of course consent to enter civil society. It is a significantly better way to live. In practice, however, no one asks us whether we wish to join society. We are assumed to have done so.

The social contract is a bargain with a specific purpose: preservation of life, liberty and property. Consequently, we owe allegiance only to those governments that achieve that purpose. Such governments have very specific obligations to their citizens. First, they must establish and make known the laws of common living—the legislative function.[30] Second, they must provide "an indifferent judge, with authority to determine all differences according to established law"—the judicial function.[31] Third, they must "back and support the sentence when right"—the executive function.[32] Locke thus proposed the division of roles among the legislature, judiciary and executive—the "separation of powers"—that characterizes the American constitutional system.

For Locke, individuals consent to a common authority in order that these three functions are carried out. Government has a very specific charge from its citizens, rather than *carte blanche* to organize society in ways that serve the interests of those who govern. In other words, the social contract is a limited bargain. Individuals do not give up all their rights to the common authority. They only give up the rights to make law, adjudicate their own disputes and enforce their own rights, that is, act as legislator, detective, arresting officer, prosecutor, judge, jury and executioner in their own case. They also give up these rights only on the condition that they receive improved security in exchange. If life under a government were less secure than life in a State of Nature (as it is for some in authoritarian states), then free, rational people would not agree to the contract.

Even if government were not cruel but merely incompetent, that is, if it were unable to provide security because it was run by weak, unintelligent or corrupt individuals, it would also fail to fulfill its obligations under the social contract. For government to provide security, it must be energetic enough to make rules and enforce them. Its representatives must be strong enough to assure that the rules are obeyed. Unless government is strong enough to protect individual rights, no one is secure.

Social contract theory is compatible with several forms of government. As long as government carries out its three central functions, it may be a democracy, an oligarchy, a monarchy (hereditary or elective) or any combination of these.[33] In Locke's version of the contract, we consent to the functions and responsibilities of government, rather than its form. Of course, in the contemporary United States, few of us would consent to anything other than a democracy.

In a democratic society, political debates sometimes revolve around whether the government has become too strong, whether too much individual liberty has been exchanged for security and whether each citizen has equal access to the benefits of government security. At other times, individuals concerned about social disorder or crime worry that government has provided for too much liberty or that criminals have too many rights. Given that liberty and security are seen as trade-offs (that is, that they are elements exchanged in a bargain), it is not surprising that each generation wishes to re-examine the terms under which the social contract is made, or that certain groups in society would question whether all members of society benefit equally from the bargain. We know, of course, that they do not, and the press for civil rights by various social groups can be understood in these terms. Indeed, Locke would encourage each individual to go through this rational exercise in allegiance.[34]

THE POLICE OFFICER AS SPORTS REFEREE: A USEFUL ANALOGY

One way to think about the role of government under Locke's conception of social contract is to think about government as if it were a referee at a sporting event, say a professional hockey or basketball game, or the umpire in major league baseball. The executive branch in particular (of which the police are a part) and sports referees share the quality of having authority and power. As referee, the executive interprets rules (the laws), enforces them and arbitrates disputes among "players" (citizens). As with referees, the public seems to enjoy booing the performance of government, but most seem to abide by its decisions.

We are introducing the referee analogy here because it is implicit in the Lockean conception of governmental function (he speaks of the government as an "Umpire") and because it helps to clarify the specific obligations of authorities to the citizenry. However, it is important to remember that this analogy only works at a very broad conceptual level. It is not an analogy that differentiates police functions from those of judges, prosecutors, prison guards, parole officers and others with authority in law enforcement organizations. The police are sometimes, literally, referees, but in many other of their functions they are not. Nevertheless, if one thinks of the laws as, in a general sense, the "rules of the game," then law enforcement has some structural similarities to refereeing.[35] The analogy is a heuristic; it permits us to think about the obligations of police in a different, but more familiar light—the obligations of sports referees. We have found this analogy especially helpful in introducing these concepts in police-training classes. The value of the comparison is that we can use our understanding of "good refereeing" to understand the elements of "good" law enforcement and to see how they are derived from the social contract perspective.

A referee's purpose is to make certain that the game is played fairly and within the rules. To achieve this end, a referee must have certain attributes and attitudes. For one, the referee must be neutral: above the game and disinterested in its outcome. He must not favor some players at the expense of others. He must not care who wins. Imagine what would happen if a basketball referee were rooting for one of the competing teams, or if the umpire calling balls and strikes had bet on the home team. Imagine a hockey referee with a prejudice against Canadian players who refused to call penalties on American players. Favoritism, prejudice and self-interest can each distort a referee's capacity to judge a game fairly.

When players feel that a referee is unfair, the contest can deteriorate so that players play and enforce their own rules, which increases their chances of getting hurt. A player who thinks that the referee is not protecting his or her interests, or is favoring the other side, will often try to even the odds by cheating, breaking the rules or retaliating against opponents he feels are getting away with unseen or uncalled violations. Sometimes we see in hockey or basketball the retaliatory punch thrown by a distraught player who feels that he was fouled but the referee was unwilling to blow the whistle on the violator. When a player believes that the referee is not neutral or fair, such retaliation is an almost inevitable result.

Put another way, the referee must maintain control over the game both to keep it flowing smoothly and to keep the players from retaliating for real or imagined fouls. That is, the referee enforces the official rules so that players refrain from imposing their private version of justice. As parties to a social contract (membership in the league implies agreement to follow the rules set by the league), players agree to give the referee a monopoly on deciding which actions are violations and which are not. If the referee cannot maintain the respect of the players, the players will challenge his or her monopoly on authority, and the crowd will "get on the referee's back," reinforcing the disrespect shown by the players. So too with governments; if they cannot maintain law and order in society, vigilante groups arise to enforce their own rights, or racketeers offer protections to those who can, or who are forced to, pay for it.

The police are the most visible government agents playing the role of social referee. Police departments and individual officers both derive their authority and power from the social contract. The contract illuminates the police role, and it also illuminates the moral obligations the police assume because of their role. As social referees, the police have power and authority like that of a sports referee: they must maintain their authority and control of the game (keeping public order); they must stay neutral and above the game (not play favorites, do special favors or receive rewards); they must enforce the rules (enforce the law); they must protect the players' interest (protect property and ensure public safety); and they must keep the players from taking the rules into their own hands (settle disputes fairly, terminate fights and prevent violence).

Just as professional sports leagues evaluate their referees each season to determine whether they are performing their duties adequately, as parties to the social contract, we are entitled to evaluate the performance of our agents (government officials in general and police in particular) in regard to their success at "refereeing" society. The perspective of the social contract allows us to derive five ethical standards from which to make moral assessments of police work. The next chapter delineates those standards, explains why they are useful for evaluating police work and explores some of the ways in which police work may or may not live up to the standards.

NOTES

1. Thomas Hobbes, *Leviathan* (New York: E.P. Dutton, 1950).
2. For an excellent account of this period, see Christopher Hill, *The Century of Revolution: 1603–1714* (New York: Norton, 1961).
3. Hobbes, p. 104.
4. John Locke, *Two Treatises of Government, A Critical Edition with an Introduction and Apparatus Criticus*, ed. Peter Laslett (Cambridge, England: Cambridge University Press, 1970).
5. Ibid.
6. Declaration of Independence.
7. Constitution of the United States.
8. *The Federalist Papers*, ed. Clinton Rossiter (New York: New American Library, 1961).
9. *Federalist Papers*, No. 15, pp. 105–13.
10. *Federalist Papers*, No. 37, pp. 224–31.
11. Locke, *Second Treatise*, Sec. 2, p. 268.
12. Ibid., Sec. 3, p. 268.
13. Ibid., Sec. 4, p. 268.
14. Ibid., Sec. 4.
15. Ibid., Sec. 6, pp. 270–71.
16. Isaiah Berlin, "Two Concepts of Liberty," *Four Essays on Liberty* (Oxford, England: Oxford University Press, 1969).
17. Locke, *Second Treatise*, Sec. 6, pp. 270–71.
18. Ibid.
19. Ibid., Sec. 8, p. 272.
20. Ibid., Sec. 16, pp. 278–79.
21. Ibid., Sec. 19, pp. 280–81.

22. Ibid., Sec. 95, pp. 330–31.
23. Ibid., Sec. 97, p. 332.
24. Ibid., Sec. 96, pp. 331–32.
25. Ibid., Sec. 97, p. 332.
26. Ibid., Sec. 119, pp. 347–48.
27. Ibid., Sec. 120, pp. 348–49.
28. Ibid., Sec. 101, p. 334.
29. Ibid., Sec. 103, pp. 335–36.
30. Ibid., Sec. 124, pp. 350–351.
31. Ibid., Sec. 125, p. 351.
32. Ibid., Sec. 126, p. 351.
33. Ibid., Sec. 132, p. 354.
34. Ibid., Sec. 94, pp. 329–30.
35. Technically speaking, referees are also like judges: they assign punishments. They function as police when they *detect* rules violations, and as judges when they assess the penalty for violations (i.e., free throws, points deducted, plays recalled, etc.). The analogy between police and referees has also been acknowledged from the other perspective. Earl Strom, a well-known professional basketball referee, is quoted as saying: "I would crouch down and look for things to happen. I was like a cop and, for some reason, people liked that." Jeff Coplon, "Profiles (Earl Strom)" *The New Yorker*, October 1, 1990.

3

Moral Standards for Police Work

Working from the perspective of the social contract, we have been able to define five ethical standards from which we can make moral assessments of police behavior. The goal of this chapter is to show why police conduct—at the individual or agency level—that lives up to these standards should be judged as good, and why behavior or policy that does not live up to them should be criticized or condemned. At the outset, we will discuss what standards are in general, and how they apply to police work in particular. Next, we will try to present the five standards in this chapter in such a way that they can clearly inform the reading of Part Two of this book. To assist you in that effort, we have reduced the standards to five key phrases that will form a basis from which you can think about what is ethically acceptable in the conduct of police officers (and, by extension, public servants in general). As we noted in the Introduction, the five standards of ethical policing are as follows: Police must (1) provide fair access to their services; (2) insure that their power is held and used as a public trust, and will not be abused; (3) put the primacy of safety and security of citizens before the unreflective enforcement of law; (4) acknowledge the coordination of governance with other officials in the system (teamwork); and (5) maintain an attitude of non-partisan objectivity in carrying out their functions. After a brief discussion of how we understand the application of these standards, we will discuss each of them in turn, stating it more fully, showing how it derives from the obligations inherent in the social contract and indicating the patterns of unethical police behavior that develop when the standards are ignored.

HOW STANDARDS WORK

Standards are the measures by which we make our judgments—including value judgments. The content of the standards define, in the case at hand, the kinds and levels of behavior that are expected of police officers given their role in society as we have expressed it in the language of the social contract. In setting standards, we create a measuring device that permits us to evaluate and judge what police say and do in particular situations. We do this because we want police behavior to "measure up" to the standards as much as possible. The standards provide a goal that we hope police would strive to meet.

There are a number of ways to think of standards, and it will be useful to outline some of them briefly here in order to clarify the ways in which the five standards listed above will be used throughout this book. Standards, in the first place, may be precise or approximate. An example of an extremely precise standard is the standard yardstick kept at the National Bureau of Standards in Washington D.C. This is the most precise "yard" we can define; a steel rod precisely thirty-six inches long is kept in a vacuum chamber free of contact with atmospheric elements that might expand, contract, corrode or deteriorate it. In order to make a truly accurate yardstick for our own use, it would be best to be able to measure and cut one that precisely matched the official yardstick in Washington D.C. Because the official standard yardstick is, by convention, exactly one yard, our ability to meet that standard with our own yardsticks is limited only by our ability to measure and cut with precision. There is nothing vague, approximate or unclear in the standard itself.

When we enter the realm of human affairs, precision begins to abandon us. There is no precise standard smile, frown, greeting or way to say "no" to another person. In all of the things people do with and to one another—giving orders, helping out, teaching, negotiating, socializing and the like—there is tremendous variation. Our standards, consequently, lose their precision. There is no standard handshake against which others can be measured. Neither is there one way to remove a drunk from a bar, calm a family dispute or conduct an investigation. There are, of course, better and worse ways to do all of these things.

We still know that a frown is not just another way to smile, beating someone senseless is not another way to negotiate and threatening a person is not a way to make him or her feel relaxed. In short, even where precision is not possible, standards may be set. Those standards, however, must accommodate variation in the behavior that meets them while distinguishing it from behavior that does not meet them. At the edges, these standards will be open to interpretation and be, in effect, approximations of what we expect of human behavior.

So far we have been looking at standards that are singular in the sense that they measure one thing only. The standard yard measures length, but not surface texture. Often we are in a position where we want to measure several qualities or characteristics of something at the same time. When this is the case, standards may become compound. A good example of a compound standard is a building code. Local governments invariably have housing codes that all construction work must measure up to: electrical wires must have a specified type of insulation, plumbing pipes must have a certain width and thickness, gas lines must be buried a certain number of feet under the ground and so on. These codes generally go on to specify literally hundreds of standards that a properly constructed building must meet. Each of these must be met individually, and all of them must be met collectively in order for a building to be up to code. Construction or repair work that does not meet or exceed the standards is in violation of the code and must be redone correctly, with a penalty to the building owner or contractor or both if the work is not brought up to standard. Housing codes are inflexible and strictly enforced, because there is a great public interest in the proper construction of buildings to keep them safe from fire, sanitary problems and other hazards. Building codes tend to be precise as well as compound, because governments do not want to give contractors the discretion to compromise safety in exchange for saving the cost of materials or labor.

Our measures of multiple characteristics of something are not always simply additive as they are in building specifications. Sometimes the characteristics we are assessing are interrelated to one another, so our evaluation is complex rather than compound. An excellent example of a complex standard is the measure of being a good hitter in baseball. Good hitting has several interacting dimensions: hitting for average, batting runs in, hitting home runs, avoiding double plays and strikeouts, "clutch" hitting and so on. Good hitting can be measured by any number of combinations of achievement in these categories. These particular dimensions can be measured with precision—.300 or better batting average, 100 or more runs batted in per season, 35 or more home runs per season and so on. Although these measurements are precise, the standards for good hitting are not. We would not say that a .300 hitter is good, but a .298 hitter is bad. The numbers do not designate absolute cutoffs. Furthermore, a .280 hitter who also drives in 110 runs and hits 30 home runs is highly rated as a hitter—perhaps more highly rated than the .310 hitter who drives in 45 runs and hits 15 home runs. Exceptional success along one dimension can compensate for weakness along another (home runs/strikeouts), and "across the board" strength can be rated more highly than spectacular performance in one area coupled with weakness in others. In short, there is no simple standard for good hitting. Despite the existence of precise measurements, the standard is approximate and complex.

STRIVING FOR VIRTUE

A final approach to thinking about standards will be important to our understanding how to measure police work. Standards may set minimum criteria for performance, or they may set ideals to reach for. The above-mentioned building codes are examples of minimum standards. A house must have at least such and such amount of insulation in its walls. Should a builder wish to double the insulation rating, he is permitted to do so. Another approach to standards is to set perfection as the ideal and to measure how close something comes to reaching it. The standards for being a "good Samaritan" fall into this category. Minimal levels of helpfulness are expected of everyone, but going out of your way to help others is the measure of a good Samaritan. How much out of your way? There is no sharp line to draw here. Good Samaritanism is an ideal to strive for. Calling the authorities about an accident you witness is expected behavior; remaining at the scene to assist is admirable; staying with the victim afterward to give comfort demonstrates even greater virtue. Yet there is, in theory, always more one might do, and the measure of a good Samaritan is taken against the maximum.

Lon L. Fuller, in *The Morality of Law*,[1] draws a distinction that captures these divergent conceptions of standards. He distinguishes the "morality of duty" from the "morality of aspiration," and presents them as two segments of a vertical line. Duty, on the lower segment, defines the minimally acceptable behavior. Aspiration constitutes the upper segment. All behavior along this upper part of the line is at least good—Fuller calls it virtuous. Yet behavior in this category can also be "better" or even "best." Virtue is an ideal to strive for. Falling short is not subject to serious moral criticism—as long as one does one's duty. Despite our occasional impatience with those who do just enough to meet their obligations, from a moral point of view, they are to be encouraged to go further rather than criticized for not doing more. Everything beyond duty is praiseworthy, and some actions are more praiseworthy than others. This distinction will be quite useful when we come to apply standards to examples of police behavior. Often there is a range of responses to a problem. Some of them are unacceptable, but others are at least good. On occasion, an officer will craft a response that is positively inspired. This can be praised without implying that other, perfectly acceptable, responses are in any way tarnished. With this in mind, let us turn to a set of standards that are approximate, complex and, on occasion, ideal.

THE FIVE STANDARDS OF ETHICAL POLICING

There are five ethical standards against which police work can be judged:

Standard I: *Fair Access*. As a social resource, police must provide fair access to their services.

Standard II: *Public Trust*. Citizens, having limited their right to enforce their own rights, have made police work a public trust.

Standard III: *Safety and Security*. Police must undertake law enforcement within the framework of maintaining safety and security.

Standard IV: *Teamwork*. Police are part of a system that includes legislators, other law enforcers, prosecutors and judges, so their behavior must meet the tests of teamwork: coordination, communication and cooperation.

Standard V: *Objectivity*. Police work is a social role that often requires the officer to set personality and feelings aside, and demonstrate objectivity.

Standard I: Fair Access

The first standard proposes that, as a shared social resource, police must provide fair access to their services. As we know from the social contract perspective, the police often function as society's referees. This means they must be available to go places where disputes, disruptions or violations of the rules may be occurring: crime scenes, domestic disturbances, accident scenes, large gatherings or noisy parties. Police must be ready to use their power and authority to restore or maintain calm. They bring force and the right to use it to those situations in which the peace and security of citizens are in jeopardy. In the language of sports, it is their job to "control" the game.

All citizens have the right to call on the police when their security is at risk, because (from the social contract perspective) all citizens have agreed to transfer to government their right to self-protection—the right to enforce their rights—in exchange for greater security. Furthermore, no individual can say, as a practical matter, that he or she is not a party to the social contract and subject to its conditions. This is a consequence of Locke's assertion that all of us, explicitly or tacitly, agree to the terms of the bargain. So the other side of equal access is equal liability. That is, no one can resist the police in the lawful performance of their duties or refuse to comply with the lawful commands of the police. It is not possible to say, when a police officer tells you to pull your car over for speeding, that the laws do not apply to you. You cannot tell the officer that you have opted not to be a member of society. Equal access and equal liability really are two sides of the same coin. My access to police service is valuable precisely because the police have authority over all who might threaten my security. Equal access asserts that each of us is entitled to the same protection.

Fair access is, of course, access to the services police are actually authorized by statute to provide. It is not the responsibility of police to bring about social equality in ways that go beyond their job descriptions. If a police officer spends time off duty coaching a basketball team of underprivileged youth, he is to be commended, but not because he is providing fair access to a group of young people. Police officers also need to be cautious about taking fair access over into the realm of compensatory justice. They ought not to create obstacles to the use of their services, but neither are they obliged to be more than decently helpful when it comes to educating citizenry about the ways they may make use of the police force. Teaching people to use social services is partly the responsibility of the social agencies, but it is also broader than that. A wise police officer will see the benefit of helping others to understand when to call the cops, but he will not let public education become his preoccupation.

Equal access does not mean constant access, or access whenever you want it. The basis upon which citizens have the right to expect police action is need of services. Citizens are not entitled to a predetermined allotment of police protection or to as much protection as they can personally afford.[2] Nor are they entitled to police services every time they feel they would like to have them—for example, to get the proverbial cat out of their tree. Each member of society is entitled to police services when, in some generalized sense, he or she needs them. To be sure, need is not a clear or simple concept. There are different kinds of need (physical, psychological), and comparisons of one kind to another are not easily accomplished. Recognizing that there is no social consensus on a ranked list of all possible needs, as a practical matter, protection of life takes precedence over security of property, security of property over a peaceful night's sleep and so on. The issues for police are actually even more complicated than this. The needs of a community (and of the members of a community) are shaped by history and context. In an area where car theft is rampant, it may be more important to track down another stolen automobile than to take a report on a relatively rare mugging. The key point here is that departments must try to assess the needs for service in their community, rank those needs and communicate that ranking to the officers who must respond to them.

Because so many people have a need for the police, and because police are not an unlimited social resource, their services must be prioritized. Problems and situations that are most disruptive to public safety or security must receive attention first. Police departments must set priorities for response patterns and limit the amount of police attention to some kinds of calls for service. The "need" for police service must be measured by the impact of police action on the security and safety of the citizenry as a whole, or on one citizen as opposed to others. As a rule, it is more important to deal with an epidemic of muggings or street crime in a neighborhood than with double parking on Main Street, but even here one might imagine circumstances that would challenge these priorities.

Within the context of a community's priorities, fair access to police services means that individuals with a relatively equal need for those services should have a relatively equal opportunity to receive them.

Need should be the only criterion for police attention. Officers should not withhold their services for reasons having to do with age, race, ethnic identification, gender, previous police history, location of the call for service, the personal likes or dislikes of the dispatcher giving out the assignment or the prejudices of the responding officer toward the persons he or she is serving. A poor person in need of help should have the same chance of receiving it as a rich person needing it—and vice versa. Modern telephone systems go a long way toward universalizing access to the police; improved forms of response, such as differential police response, rapid response to crime-in-progress calls and specially trained rape crisis or domestic violence intervention units, are innovative means at the departmental level to address the issue of providing priority service on a fair-access basis.

Fair access to public resources is one basis of social justice, and it is a main way in which police affect the quality of justice in society. By apprehending those who injure others or calming those who threaten the peace, police provide society at large with access to safety, order and security. To the degree that we cannot gain fair access to their services, the police deprive at least some of us of the benefits for which, in Locke's terms, we have formed civil society.

If fair access is a measure of good police work, it becomes possible to define ways in which police behavior fails to meet this standard. There are, of course, more and less scrupulous attempts at being fair, all of which fall into the realm of virtue. However, there are also minimal standards of fairness. Officers risk abusing fair access when they engage in favoritism and when they neglect the needs of certain groups.

Favoritism

Favoritism occurs when an officer selects, through invalid or invidious distinctions, some individuals or groups for special attention and offers them better access to his or her services. A merchant benefits disproportionately from police favoritism when an officer, acting out of friendship or for some reward rather than on official orders, accompanies the merchant to make bank deposits. Similarly, individual businesses in high-crime areas benefit from disproportionate police presence if an officer chooses to spend a significant amount of time in the establishment or if the officer agrees at the request of the owner to make special patrols to watch the place of business. This kind of favoritism has the additional problem of tempting the merchant to offer gratuities—discounts or gifts—to attract or sustain the officer's special attention. Without argument, the merchant receiving these favors may actually need the officer's presence or his services. What is important here is that the merchant has imposed his own priority, rather than society's broader needs or the police department's priorities, on the individual officer's use of time, which is, after all, a public resource to which all are equally entitled.

Another kind of favoritism is the kind that offers special dispensation to friends or fellow officers. When an officer gives some people immunities from speeding tickets or from arrest for drunk driving or gambling because those individuals are co-workers, relatives, friends or merely members of the same profession, that officer is violating the standard of fair access. Others who might perform the same actions do not have the same immunity from the consequences of their actions. Put another way, favoritism means that privileged individuals favored by the police have less to fear from violating some laws than others who violate the same laws.[3]

Neglect

The second major violation of the fair-access standard is neglect. Groups can be victimized by neglect when departments or groups of officers make no effort to serve particular neighborhoods, housing developments or racial or ethnic communities. Sometimes a neighborhood or public-housing development will develop a reputation among officers as hopeless, dangerous or unappreciative, and some officers may avoid providing service there or be slow in responding to calls from there. Some officers may avoid groups (like Southeast Asian or Haitian immigrants) who are culturally distinct, not well understood or who have a limited ability to communicate in English, because the officers may feel bewildered by contacts with them.

Another form of neglect depends less on the character of the group or neighborhood than on the character of the officer. Some officers are what William Ker Muir, Jr.[4] has called "avoiders"; they try to keep from getting involved in the risks inherent in police work. They are not assertive, often feel afraid or incompetent to deal with hostile individuals and have no desire to be helpful. When possible, they find ways to cut short their contacts with the public, avoid meeting their supervisors while doing their work and rationalize their refusal to give service on the grounds that the matter in question is not one for the police. Avoider officers define such things as landlord–tenant disputes or family arguments as civil court matters, rowdy juveniles on a bus as a concern for the transit authority or drug dealing or prostitution in poor neighborhoods as forms of local business rather than as a crime problem for respectable residents. These officers, by their inactivity, deny fair access to police services to those who call on them in time of need or crisis, or who have a legitimate expectation that the police will help them deal with their problems.

The fair-access standard, then, demands that police officers shall make themselves available to the public on the basis of the public's need for services. Their personal decisions about the use of their time should be guided by departmental and community priorities, and not by favoritism toward some groups or individuals and neglect of others. This is an approximate standard that is based, first, on the principle of justice: treat similar cases similarly unless and until there is a reason to do otherwise, but, second, the standard can be made more precise through departmental and community articulation of its law enforcement and service priorities.

Standard II: Public Trust

Standard II specifies that citizens, having limited their right to enforce their own rights, have made police work a public trust. Let us acknowledge at the outset that nothing in this standard strips the individual citizen of his or her right of immediate self-defense. If I am being attacked by a person with a club, I am permitted to pick up a club, knife or gun to protect myself. I do not have to summon the police and passively take a beating until they arrive. By saying that citizens have limited their right to enforce their rights, we mean only that citizens have, because they live voluntarily under the terms of the social contract, abandoned their right to serve as prosecutor, judge and jury in disputes or conflicts to which they are a party. The government, as we have noted, is society's referee, beginning with the police, as are, by extension, the prosecutor and the courts.

The following example illustrates this point. Should I return home from work one evening and find that my television has been stolen and that the thief is no longer on the premises, I am not permitted to pick up a stick or gun and force my way into my neighbor's home to search for my property. Instead, if I want to restore my loss and have the satisfaction of seeing someone punished for her misdeeds, I must depend upon the criminal justice system. In this case, I start by "calling the cops," who will come (according to their availability) to investigate the crime. Even if I had looked through the window of the house next door and saw my television sitting on the kitchen table, leading me to the overwhelming conviction that the juvenile delinquent living next door had stolen it, I cannot enter her house to retrieve my television without her permission. With a warrant, a police officer can do that on my behalf. The difference between the officer and me is that the officer is authorized to secure a warrant and intrude himself on crime suspects, whereas as a private citizen I am not. As a member of civil society who is a party to the social contract, I transferred this right to perform law enforcement to the police.

Because they are authorized to use force or coerce citizens on behalf of all citizens who are prohibited from doing this for themselves, police officers—in fact, all agents of the criminal justice system—exercise their powers in trust for the citizenry.[5] Transferring their enforcement powers to the police is thus an act of trust on the part of the public: they trust that the police will act on their behalf, and have faith that, when they telephone for police assistance, someone will respond helpfully. As referees, the police must enforce the rules to protect all the players in the game.

The public authorizes the police to use its power for the public's own sake, in its defense and on its behalf. The public gives police the authority to enter places thought to be the scenes of crimes, with and without warrants. It gives them the right to stop and search persons who might be dangerous to others (as long as they have probable cause to do so). It gives them the right in the course of performing their authorized functions to restrain those who would inflict pain and harm on others. These actions must, of course, be justifiable—and they often must be justified in a report after the fact. However, the key point here is that the police are public agents who take actions that are no longer permitted to private citizens. Remembering the logic of the social contract, we know that, if each of us were to continue exercising these powers for ourselves, life would soon deteriorate into a paranoid war of "all against all" in which every person with his hand in his pocket would be perceived as a potential threat to us.

Although the notion that the police hold and exercise our rights in trust for us is one meaning of the term "public trust," that term also has a second dimension. This refers to the fact that the police are permitted to be more powerful than other citizens.[6] Because police are authorized to use force and coercion to maintain public order and safety, their lawful commands override the desire of any individual citizen to do what he or she pleases. Because they represent the interests of society as a whole in the maintenance of order, they have the right (in the appropriate circumstances) to command any one of us to move along, to stop, to desist from a certain behavior or to come along with them against our will.

Conversely, we have no lawful right to resist the lawful commands of a police officer. We may choose to do so, but police officers are authorized to overcome our resistance. The police, in Egon Bittner's words, are the bearers of non-negotiable force.[7] It is their social function to exercise an authority, and to do so on behalf of all of us, that need not be justified in order for them to do their work. Because the point of police action is often the resolution of a conflict, we ought not to question their lawful decisions (although often we do exactly that), and they need not stop to explain to us why they have made a decision they consider within their authority and the public interest. Few if any persons in our society are as powerful as the police when they are handling an emergency or a crime. Not even parents have this breadth of authority over their children.

Trust and Restraint

Pointing to this powerfulness in police also points us to the second layer of connection between the police and the public trust. Because their lawful uses of authority may not lawfully be resisted by citizens, police officers are obligated to exercise great restraint in their use of it. Think particularly of those cases in which a citizen *does* resist the lawful use of authority by an officer, as in the following example:

An officer approaches and questions an obviously intoxicated man who is bothering several families and groups of friends in a public park. When the officer requests that the drunk leave the park, he throws a beer bottle at the officer, calls him a number of dirty names and tells the officer he will have to fight him like a man to get him to leave.

When the drunk resisted the officer's lawful command physically and in a dangerous way, the officer was justified in subduing the drunk by whatever appropriate means were necessary, including force and arrest. The drunk can be considered a threat to himself, the officer and those around him, since his judgment is clouded by alcohol (evidence for which is the fact that he thinks he can fight the officer). The drunk might also escalate his attacks on the officer, following up the tossed bottle by pulling a concealed weapon, or by trying to grab the officer's stick or gun.

Despite the dangers that the drunk poses, we expect the officer to use great restraint in handling him. After all, a drunk is usually not supposed to be a match for a well-trained, sober police officer. If they wrestle, the officer should be the odds-on favorite to win, since he has his senses about him and is normally well trained and in better physical shape than most citizens. If the drunk should pull a stick, club or knife, the officer can defend himself with his nightstick, if he so chooses, and might, depending on circumstances, even be justified in pulling his gun. Should the drunk pull a gun, the officer is expected to be the better trained and more experienced shot, and to have an aim undistorted by the effects of alcohol. We realize, to be sure, that in practice the officer does not always have the upper hand. Not every officer is in excellent physical shape, an expert marksman and fully alert to danger. Life does not always mirror the textbook. For the most part, however, even though they are flesh and blood humans, police are more powerful than "mere" citizens. Because they have authority over others and are given the training in how to exercise it, we hold them to a high standard in its use. Police must do minimum harm in the use of their public authority. We ask them to apply the minimum necessary force to accomplish their tasks.

Because we cannot lawfully resist the police,[8] we must depend on them not to harm us unnecessarily (as opposed to never harm us in any circumstances). To return to the case of the drunk in the park, the officer is expected to make a judgment about the minimum necessary force that is needed to defend himself and others from the drunk, and to remove the drunk from the scene while inflicting the least amount of pain and harm on the drunk consistent with getting the job done. This does not preclude shooting and killing the drunk if circumstances warrant (e.g., if the drunk pulled a gun himself). The force, after all, must be necessary as well as minimal. However, this level of force could hardly be justified simply by the act of the drunk's having thrown a bottle. The officer owes it to the drunk, to bystanders and to society at large to attempt to subdue that drunk without threatening his life or causing serious injury, if at all possible. Talk would be best; force may surely be used if in the officer's judgment it is necessary, as long as it is used in minimum doses and as a last resort. After all, we created police authority to preserve life (even the lives of those who threaten others, when possible) and not to place it at the mercy of a police officer's whim.[9]

Trust and Corruption

The connection between power, authority and the public trust has yet another dimension. Officers have the opportunity to use the power created by their public authority for private or personal gain. For example, it used to be a fairly common practice (we do not hear of it as much in recent times) for some police officers to stop motorists for traffic violations with the expectation that the motorist would offer cash or other rewards in exchange for the officer not writing a citation. Some officers make drug arrests with the expectation of keeping some of the dealers' money, drugs or both. Some threaten to arrest prostitutes if they do not bestow sexual favors on the officers. Others expect to be rewarded for providing the benefits of their presence, such as officers who patronize particular restaurants or coffee shops because they are given free or discount food if they appear in uniform. What all these practices have in common is that an officer is using his public authority (the power to enforce or not enforce the law at his discretion) as a way to advance his private monetary interests.[10]

Although it is obvious that police officers should not "shake down" motorists for bribes in exchange for letting them escape written citations, it is less clear that police officers should not accept a cup of coffee if it is freely offered by a grateful doughnut shop owner whose premises are open all night in a high-crime area. Later on we will examine the ethics of the free cup of coffee. We cite it now as a way to ask what it means to exercise a public trust. Like the referee who should not bet on the outcome of the game, a public police badge must not be used for private gain. As Patrick Murphy, former police commissioner of New York City and president of the Police Foundation, once explained to his fellow officers, "except for your paycheck, there's no such thing as a clean buck."[11]

In sum, the public trust standard asserts that police exercise their authority on behalf, and in the name, of citizens. Because citizens have made themselves vulnerable by relinquishing the right to resist the police, this standard requires that police exercise their acquired authority with restraint. To the extent that departments set policy on the use of minimal necessary force, they make this standard more precise. The concept of public trust also emphasizes that this standard prohibits private gain at public expense. Here too the department can set policy (such as with respect to accepting gratuities and rewards) in order to make the standard a more precise measuring tool.

Standard III: Safety and Security

The third standard requires the police to undertake law enforcement within the framework of maintaining safety and security. This is a standard that requires the police to develop and exercise good judgment, and particularly relates to the use of such practices as arrest, stopping and questioning or searching citizens and other coercive means in the enforcement of laws. Put another way, this standard seeks to provide some answers to the question of what the police mission is and how officers can accomplish that mission in their work.

It is almost always justified per se for the police to enforce the law when it is broken in their presence. After all, police are sworn under oath to uphold it. Under the terms of the social contract, law is society's set of rules governing common life. These rules are, on their face, in everyone's long-term interest to support (even if it is in someone's short-term interest to break them), and the police are empowered by us to uphold these rules in our name. For the police to neglect to enforce a law when it is violated in their presence may seem to some a mockery of the social contract and a violation of the public trust, as well as a violation of their oath of office. Such omission might also seem unfair to those against whom the same law had been enforced previously or those against whom it will be enforced in the future. If the players see the referee overlook a foul, the victims will feel themselves wronged, and the violator will see himself or herself as immune.

On the other hand, it may be unwise for the police to enforce every law they see violated in their presence or whose violation they might know about. An obvious example comes to mind. In all of the United States except Nevada and New Jersey, it is against the law to gamble on a card game or dice game. Yet every evening, in every American city and town, literally hundreds of thousands of American men and women play games, such as poker, craps, blackjack, mah jongg, canasta, hearts and bridge, for small or large stakes. Churches and other organizations hold public bingo games or Las Vegas nights. Rather than seek warrants and arrest all those who play a friendly game among themselves or who play at respectable places, such as churches or VFW halls, police limit their enforcement of the anti-gambling statutes to those games that are played in alleyways or the back of public barrooms. It is in games in which the "house" takes a "cut," in which the players are strangers to each other and in which they might possibly behave in a hostile or threatening fashion should they lose that the police see a potential threat. To intrude in a friendly game among respectable friends or neighbors in the home of one of the players would require a level of intrusiveness into citizens' privacy that most of us would not tolerate; we would see such police activity as a violation of our rights even though, technically, we had been breaking the law. What must be balanced here is the need to uphold the law and keep the peace, on the one hand, with maintaining citizens' sense of security about the privacy of their homes and freedom of association on the other. In this case, maintaining the sense of security about privacy rights seems to outweigh the imperative to enforce the law. Indeed, enforcing the gambling laws rigorously and thoroughly would have the likely effect of undermining the sense of order and security that is the primary purpose of law enforcement.

There might well be times when making an arrest or issuing a citation outweighs other considerations, including those of (relative) public safety. Issues of "hot pursuit" and high-speed chases can be seen in this light. Hot pursuit has been a subject of considerable discussion in police circles, and the hard cases remain a puzzle. In general, the interests of citizen safety and security are in ascendancy over strict law enforcement; however, there are cases where public safety may seem best served in the long run if it is ignored in the short run. Suppose armed bank robbers are fleeing in an automobile and have taken a bank teller as hostage. Officers arriving in response to a silent alarm spot the fleeing robbers and decide to chase them. The streets are relatively crowded with other cars and many bystanders. The robbers spot the police cars and start to fire bullets at them. The pursuing officers must make a decision—or their supervisors must make it for them—whether to continue pursuing the fleeing robbers. On the one hand, if they call off the chase, the robbers will no longer have a reason to be firing the shots that endanger innocent citizens walking along the streets or in passing vehicles. On the other, the robbers would escape with their hostage, whose life may be in immediate danger if the robbers are not apprehended quickly. In this case, the potential risks to passersby and the officers may be outweighed by the pressing threat to the hostage; pursuit by the officers may be justifiable despite the threat of such tactics to public safety.

Such difficult balances between safety on the one hand and law enforcement on the other can be assessed through reference to the terms of the social contract. As Locke argued, individuals create civil society to advance their personal physical safety and the security of their property. Laws are a tool for enhancing that safety and security; law enforcement is a technique by which police officers and other criminal justice officials maintain public order. In this sense, law enforcement is a means; the maintenance of order and security is the end that those means serve. As Locke indicated, the purpose of living under the social contract is increased security, not simply the desire to live under rules for their own sake.

If law enforcement threatens security or individual rights (as it would if the police entered private homes to break up friendly card games, to see who kept pornographic pictures under their beds, or to look for books espousing unpopular political philosophies), then none of us would be secure in the long run from government's overextension of its authority. In this regard, *overzealous enforcement* is the most serious abuse of Standard III. If the police undertake a high-speed chase of a car that teenagers have taken for a joyride and that chase ends with the kids or cops crashing into a tree, or crashing into another car, then enforcing the law against joyriding or speeding is hardly worth the consequences. Overzealous enforcement of law can cross the line that makes life less secure even for the law-abiding.

On the other hand, enunciating policies that prohibit the police from enforcing the law whenever citizens are at some risk because of its enforcement can have the unintended effect of enticing criminals to take hostages routinely or always to make high-speed escape attempts. Thus, at the level of policy as well as performance, in circumstances where law and safety are in potential conflict, police must strike a balance between enforcing the law, as they are sworn to do, and providing for public safety, which may involve forgoing law enforcement. Standard III, *safety and security*, specifies that the balance must be struck not as a compromise between two competing goals, but as an ordering of means (law enforcement) to ends (safety and security). This standard articulates a direction for law enforcement, and marks a limit where overzealous or thoughtless police action fails to measure up.

Standard IV: Teamwork

As part of the criminal justice system, police officers and organizations are part of a governmental structure of other enforcers, prosecutors and judges that requires their behavior to meet the tests of *teamwork*: coordination, communication and cooperation.

The social contract identifies three functions of government: legislative, executive and judicial. Although it is possible that all three of these functions could be placed in the hands of a single agency, in our system of government they are not. We call this division of function the separation of powers. The purpose of the separation of powers is to provide checks on each government agency by other agencies, so that no one agency becomes so powerful that it can put the liberty and security of the citizenry in jeopardy. Separation of powers helps assure that each citizen receives "due process of law." Thus, the occasional conflict among the branches is appropriately built into the criminal justice system.

In the United States, the police are defined as an (but not the only) enforcement arm of the executive branch of government. Functions such as prosecuting and judging (except for the least significant of crimes) are left to other agencies or branches of government. Thus, to be effective in protecting society against criminal behavior, the police must coordinate their efforts with, communicate with and cooperate with other elements of the executive branch (for example, they must give clear reports to and preserve evidence for prosecutors), with the legislature (to convince them to pass or amend laws) and with the judiciary (by testifying clearly and honestly under oath).

Furthermore, police work cannot be accomplished most effectively one-on-one. Although it is true that incidents and disruptions must be handled one at a time, the quality of police services that a community receives depends on the patterns of enforcement and the consistency of response of its entire police department. There may be better or worse individual officers, but the police reputation in a community is the reputation of a department. The effectiveness of each officer depends on the effectiveness of his or her partner (if he or she has one), squad, supervisor(s) and chief. No officer can accomplish the goals of police work—providing safety and security to citizens while enforcing the law—without the cooperation and support of other officers and civilian employees of the police department. Nor can one department operate effectively without cooperating with neighboring departments and state and federal law enforcement agencies. An individual officer might do the best possible job on her own, but without an effective departmental organization and interagency cooperation, her most outstanding efforts are unlikely to have lasting impact.

If a department is to be effective, then each officer in it has an obligation to act as part of a team, and give the cooperation that he or she expects to receive in return. Teamwork is a two-way street. Each officer has a right to expect it and a duty to give it. This sense of teamwork applies not only to relations within the department—with fellow officers, members of other bureaus or divisions and with supervisors and commanders—but with members of other departments or agencies who might benefit from sharing information.

Because the success of the police function depends on teamwork, police behavior that tends to undermine other officers or other actors in the system cannot measure up to moral standards. Thus, some well-known police practices—street justice, hotdogging, closing ranks—are abuses of teamwork.

Street Justice

This practice occurs when officers go beyond their function as law enforcers, and encroach on the domain of prosecutors and judges. They do this whenever they make a judgment that a suspect is guilty and then impose an informal, personally administered punishment on him or her. Informal punishments come in many forms, some of which are more objectionable than others. For example, it is technically street justice when an officer makes a group of underage teenagers pour out their beer rather than confiscating the beer and submitting it as evidence in a court of law. However, few "victims" of this street justice would object to this treatment and prefer the arrest. Nor would most of us support the idea that police should always arrest underage beer drinkers. Nevertheless, police practice in this area is not merely for police to decide. Prosecutors and the courts (and ultimately the community) should have something to say about the priority attached to processing underage violators of the alcoholic beverage laws.

More objectionable is the tendency of some officers to succumb to the temptation to rough up a prisoner or non-cooperative person in order to teach him "a lesson" or "respect for the police." Perhaps the greatest temptation to punch a suspect or tighten the handcuffs so they hurt comes when a suspect resists arrest or defies an officer's authority in a matter that a prosecutor, judge or jury is not likely to treat as "serious" (for example, during a drunk and disorderly arrest, or an arrest for disturbing the peace). If an officer decides that the suspect "deserves" punishment as a certainty, he has two options: file more serious charges (even if false), such as assault and battery on a police officer, so that the prosecutor has to try the case, or to inflict the punishment himself through a punch, a kick, overly tight handcuffs, tossing the arrestee roughly into the patrol car and so forth. Some people argue that arresting a disorderly person, rather than just warning him and letting him go, is itself a punishment because of the humiliation, trouble and expense it will cause the arrestee.

These officer-imposed punishments violate the standard of teamwork. Charging the suspect with excessive violations deprives the prosecutor and the courts of the chance to reach a fair determination of prosecutability, guilt and punishment. Often, such cases result in the officer dropping the charges in exchange for the citizen not filing a complaint against the officer (be it real or fabricated); thus justice is done to neither side. For a police officer to reserve these judgments and actions for himself or herself makes the society in which we live less safe for the individual. It is this very insecurity of life and limb that the social contract was meant to combat. By communicating charges against the accused to the prosecutor rather than becoming prosecutor, judge and jury in the case, the officer is cooperating with the criminal justice system to impose a more widely accepted definition of justice. After all, the social contract and the Constitution deprive all of us, even the police, of the right to serve as judge, jury and prosecutor in our own cases.

"Hotdogging"

In police work, as in sports, hotdogging is excessive grandstanding, going for the attention and the glory for oneself or one's department at the expense of collaborative efforts to solve public problems or crimes.

This phenomenon is sometimes seen among detectives who, looking for the "big" arrest, will not share information with other detectives or with the patrol division of their department. It has also been commonplace for local departments not to cooperate among themselves or with state or federal law enforcement agencies when working on a "major" case. Sometimes, patrol officers developing evidence against a drug dealer or gambler will not share it with officers who cover their beat on other shifts, or with detectives, because they want to make the "bust" themselves.

Partly, the media play a role in generating this competition for exclusivity; departments want the credit for breaking the major drug or car-theft ring, because it makes for exposure on the evening news. Individual officers want the "good" arrest, because it adds to the officer's "stats" and may lead to a promotion to the detective division. These desires can be minor vices, unless in pursuing their satisfaction officers and departments fail to cooperate with others at the clear expense of losing the case. Simply put, the purpose of the police is to make society safer than it would be without their existence. It is not to provide glory or career opportunities for police officers or administrators.

Closing Ranks

The third violation of the teamwork standard, closing ranks, is the opposite of hotdogging. Rather than the officer denying his or her mutual dependence on other officers, closing ranks carries the notion of teamwork or mutual dependency too far. It is loyalty to fellow officers without limits.

Police work requires loyalty to fellow officers precisely because officers are so dependent on one another in order to be effective in their jobs. They are also, to a degree, dependent on each other for their safety: they provide each other with "backup" both on and off duty. Thus, to a point, a willingness to support each other even at some risk to oneself is a necessary characteristic of police life and an important component of teamwork. Disloyalty, an unwillingness to dedicate oneself to the safety and effectiveness of other officers, can undermine a department's effectiveness and place one's fellow officers at some risk.

However, excessive loyalty is also a danger. Sometimes in the name of loyalty officers are asked to remain silent about, or participate in, practices that are illegal, immoral or socially harmful. Taking or soliciting payoffs not to enforce the law, participating in criminal conspiracies and using excessive force are practices that are themselves immoral by standards we have already examined. The refusal of others—even those who do not participate in these practices directly—to expose them or put a stop to them is also a violation of moral standards, since it undermines the effectiveness of the police function.

Silence in the name of loyalty can isolate a department from the rest of the criminal justice system and the public it is charged to protect. If an officer knows that a fellow officer is sleeping on duty, he may argue that it is his supervisor's duty to catch the sleeper. To the degree that the sleeping officer is a threat to the public's safety, however, every officer has the obligation to see that he performs his duty (after all, officers take an oath to protect the public and are trusted to so do under the terms of the social contract). Similarly, to the degree that a sleeping officer is a threat to the safety of fellow officers (should he fail to respond to a call for backup), they owe it to themselves to get the officer to carry his weight. Although it might be unrealistic to expect officers to report each other for a violation of this sort, we raise it as a way to show how teamwork applies even to this form of widely tolerated peer-group conduct.

The purpose of teamwork and the value of loyalty reside in their contributions to the effectiveness of the police in protecting the liberty and security of the public. In other words, they are means to higher ends. Closing ranks around malpractice and dishonesty has the effect of making the public less secure by making the police organization and its members less accountable and less willing to look closely at its problems (for fear of what it may find). Hotdogging makes it less effective. Street justice makes it less responsible for protecting legal rights. In sum, each of these violations has the effect of undermining the values of teamwork.

Standard V: Objectivity

As we have seen, from the perspective of the social contract, police are sometimes expected to function as society's referees. In this role, they are supposed to enforce the law in a fair and even-handed manner. It is especially important that the public perceives them to be fair, to act without particular favoritism and to act without taking advantage of their powerful position. From the perspective of the citizen, the more objective and detached the officer, the more credibly he or she fills the role. The more emotional and personal the officer, the less the officer will seem like a referee. Thus, Standard V states: Police work is a social role that often requires the officer to set personality and feelings aside, and demonstrate objectivity. By objectivity we mean to be neither overinvolved or cynical.

In stressful circumstances, anyone has difficulty remaining objective. Often, police officers are called to the scene of angry disputes or irreconcilable conflicts. Egon Bittner[12] identifies these impasses as the primary reason Americans "call the cops." Usually both sides to a dispute, for example, two motorists who have had a collision or two neighbors arguing about how loud a stereo was playing, try to convince the officer to accept their own versions of the situation. The police must deal with each person's angry feelings as well as the facts of the case. Sometimes, the parties are rude or offensive to the officer even though he or she is there to help them. Sometimes, the officer has prior knowledge of, or a relationship to, one of the parties involved.

In such cases, regardless of who the officer may think has the better case, he or she tries not to appear to choose sides or to favor personal acquaintances over others. The appearance of such unfairness will create a sense of injustice in the party not favored, which can have several consequences. The person not backed up by the officer may feel that she is not getting a good deal under the terms of the social contract, since her agent, the police officer, is failing to uphold her rights. Perceiving police "unfairness" might induce the "loser" of the argument to "take matters into her own hands," since the law, in the person of the officer, appears to operate unfairly against her interests. Choosing sides might make an enemy for the police, making it more difficult for other members of the police or criminal justice system to deal with the disaffected individual. At a minimum, the disaffected party might contribute to creating a bad reputation for the police department in the community. Again, as referee, the officer must appear to be neutral, not a partisan of one team or player.

Yet, it is very difficult for police officers, as human beings, to maintain their objectivity in all the difficult situations they must confront. Police are asked to manage situations and individuals who would make anyone angry enough to lose his or her objectivity. They must deal with spouse abusers and child molesters. Sometimes victims are particularly obnoxious, and the officer may feel no desire to offer the protection that the situation may warrant. Police officers occasionally get battered, spit upon, called obscene names, threatened and provoked. These are situations that would call up anger and a desire to retaliate in any of us. In such circumstances, we expect individuals to become upset, and we tend to excuse their strong reactions.

However, we are not so willing to excuse police for losing control in these situations. As society's "referees," police are expected to see that all of the procedural rules regarding arrest and custody are followed. We expect them not to apply unnecessary force. It takes a clear head to assure against procedural irregularities in the detention of a violent, abusive or dangerous person. An enraged officer making an arrest decreases the chances of bringing such a person to justice—other than the illegal "street justice" he or she may inflict. Participants on the scene do not bear responsibility for making the criminal justice system work, so they are not held to the same standard of accountability or conduct that applies to police officers.

Objectivity is owed to citizens, but it is a standard that creates a narrow ideal as a measure. Departures from objectivity can fall on two sides of this ideal orientation toward police work. On the one side is *overinvolvement*: caring too much about the participants in a situation and identifying with favorites. On the other is *cynicism*: caring not at all about the participants and ignoring their need to be treated attentively.

Overinvolvement

This form of policing stems from an officer's excessive aspiration to do good or to help others. In a sense, it is a vice of naïveté. Many officers begin their careers with a sincere desire "to help people" or to perform "public service." Indeed, we expect that anyone who wanted to be a police officer but had no interest in service would be a candidate for early burnout. Desire for involvement with others is a necessary ingredient of police work. One would hope that officers would never lose this desire and that they would never turn their occupation into "just a job for a paycheck." Idealism can sustain an officer through difficult ordeals, keep his faith in human nature refreshed and prevent him from falling into behaviors such as corruption or brutality. It is when this desire is untempered that it can become a problem.

There is danger in approaching police work with an excessive desire to help people. Muir[13] has observed that some officers enter their careers with an expectation that every situation will have a "good guy" and a "bad guy." He labels such officers "rescuers." Such an officer will

usually respond to events such as family disputes with a prece
notion that all husbands are batterers or that all truants and ru
are bad kids. Sometimes, one finds that the child has fled from home
because she is the victim of abuse, or that it is the husband in the arguing
couple who has been assaulted by the wife. Objectivity would allow an
officer the distance to see the situation clearly rather than prejudging it
unfairly. It also keeps the officer from overinvesting in a particular
solution to a chronic problem that he or she cannot effectuate with the
time and resources available. Therapists and social workers more appropriately mobilize resources to solve chronic family or school problems that officers have fewer resources to solve.

Given the fact that citizens sometimes "call the cops" for less than
noble purposes, or that they present officers with unsavory situations
and contacts, many young officers soon lose their desire to help people.
For example, it is difficult to want to help either party in an argument
when both are being stubborn and unreasonable, or when an officer
discovers that the party who called the police for assistance was simply
trying to intimidate the other party into submitting to his or her whim.
Police work can often lead a person into disillusionment about human
nature. Excessive overinvolvement, a desire to find a "good guy" in
every case, can become transformed into its opposite: a viewpoint that,
among those the police deal with, there are *no* good guys, only various
degrees of bad actors and troublemakers.

Cynicism

When an officer's idealistic overinvolvement is burned out, it is often
replaced by its opposite: cynicism. After they have faced too many
situations in which all parties were acting badly, officers may develop
an attitude of indifference to the persons they deal with. Rather than
simply hold one's personal feelings in check, which would accord with
the standard of objectivity, officers can begin to refuse to care about
victims. To protect themselves from getting overinvolved and disap-
pointed in their inabilities to effect a solution to chronic problems, such
as marital disputes, muggings, child abuse, teen gangs, political corruption or favoritism, officers sometimes retreat into a lack of involvement or compassion for the plight of others.

Such officers become Muir's "avoiders." The officer begins to see
those who call the police for services as disturbers of his peace. Their
appeals for help become intrusions on his time.[14] The officer comes to

see chronic problems, such as marital disputes, as insoluble and thus not worth his efforts. He starts to define "family trouble" calls as the responsibility of social agencies rather than the police. Avoiders begin to respond to these calls slowly, hoping the argument will have resolved itself before their arrival. They come to see barroom fights among minority groups as "something those people like to do," and for which there is no point in officers exerting themselves or taking risks on behalf of the participants. Landlord–tenant disputes become "civil matters" to work out in court, not part of police responsibility.

In short, the avoider becomes dead on his feet, willing to define more and more conflicts and dangerous situations as something other than "real police work"—something for social agencies or other branches of government to deal with. This attitude leaves those most at risk of injury or harm most vulnerable because the police—the agents most immediately responsible for distributing the socially created resource of public safety and protection—are slow and reluctant to provide service. For those who are served by burned out officers, life reverts to the insecurity of Locke's State of Nature.

Cynicism can lead not just to underinvolvement but to brutality. Officers who develop a cynical view of human nature can easily divide human beings into two categories: "them and us," the "good guys and the bad guys," the "law abiders and the law breakers."[15] The officer's non-objective analysis of his experiences in poor or high-crime areas has "taught" him that behaviors are common in those neighborhoods that are rarely if ever seen in his own: selling street drugs, purse snatchings, beatings and so forth. It is a relatively short step to seeing all the residents of such areas as distinctively different from those living in "respectable" neighborhoods. As a distinct species, residents of poor or high-crime areas who come into contact with the police may be treated as less-than-human: as animals or other subhuman species who "only understand force" or "deserve what they get" when they are treated brutally. Excessive force or brutal treatment is a violation of the public trust standard; when it is based on cynical or biased attitudes stemming from underinvolvement or burnout, it is also a violation of *objectivity*.

SUMMARY

We have identified five standards of police behavior, each deriving from the police role as conceptualized through the social contract. Each of these standards permits us to see why some police practices are unacceptable and why others are required. These standards help us to articulate an area of duty—minimum expectations for officer behavior. They will also help us to articulate an area of virtue—preferred solutions to difficult problems. Unfortunately, they will not permit us to generate a simple list of good police practices. That is because good policing is a complex rather than a compound activity. Efforts to fulfill each standard can affect success at fulfilling the others. We must bear in mind that police action in any given situation may be measured against several standards at once. As we noted above, the use of excessive force may be measured against both *public trust* and *objectivity*.

This last point provides a useful transition to the next section of this book, in which we apply the five standards just reviewed to several fundamental situations and dilemmas in police work. We will find that, like good hitting in baseball, more than one standard applies to each of the scenarios we present for your consideration, and the quality of the choice you make from among your options must be judged by the application of a complex set of interrelated measures. By looking carefully at difficult cases and reasoning out the morality of police behavior, you can better understand the full meaning of the measures we have just described. You will also begin to develop a grasp of professionalism in police work, and see how professionalism and morality intersect.

NOTES

1. Lon L. Fuller, *The Morality of Law*, revised ed. (New Haven: Yale University Press, 1969), pp. 5–8.

2. Of course, this statement applies only to public police resources. Citizens may engage private security or hire public police officers for private duty, both of which operate on a fee-for-service, ability-to-pay basis.

3. Some officers argue for special consideration for fellow officers on the grounds that the consequences of a drunk-driving arrest are much more severe for police than for other citizens. They cite the specter of potential loss of employment as a reason to give other officers a break. In their view, the officer's likely punishment is out of proportion to his or her crime. Even if this is true, it has its own problems—a good referee does not exempt some players from the rules or hold some players to a lower standard than others.

4. William Ker Muir, Jr., *Police: Streetcorner Politicians* (Chicago: University of Chicago Press, 1977), pp. 55–57.

5. This idea was expressed by Abraham Lincoln as government "of the people, by the people and for the people."

6. To say that the police are more powerful than other citizens is not simply to make an observation about their strength. Being most powerful is a commitment to provide the resources it takes—training, weapons, numbers—to be most powerful in a given situation. If in a given situation the police are not, in fact, most powerful, they will send reinforcements until they are.

7. Quoted in Jerome H. Skolnick and Thomas C. Gray, *Police in America* (Boston: Little, Brown, 1975), p. 67.

8. If a citizen feels unjustly or falsely arrested, he or she must nevertheless not resist. Rather, the citizen must hold his or her objections until he or she can obtain the services of a lawyer.

9. One of the most creative uses of force we know of in this regard is related by an officer who was called upon to deal with a person who thought he was Dracula and was terrorizing people in a park by attempting to bite them in the neck. The officer held out his flashlight to the deluded vampire and announced that light kills vampires. He ordered Dracula into the back of the cruiser with the threat that he would otherwise shine the light at him.

10. Howard Cohen, "Exploiting Police Authority," *Criminal Justice Ethics* 2, no. 2, (Summer/Fall, 1986), pp. 23–31.

11. Quoted in Michael Feldberg, "Gratuities, Corruption and the Democratic Ethos of Policing: The Case of the Free Cup of Coffee," *Moral Issues in Police Work*, Frederick Elliston and Michael Feldberg, eds., (Totowa, N.J.: Rowman and Allanheld, 1985), p. 267.

12. Egon Bittner, quoted in Skolnick and Gray, *Police in America*, p. 63.

13. Muir, *Police: Streetcorner Politician*, pp. 88–89.

14. Ibid., pp. 56–57.

15. Ibid., pp. 22–25.

Part II

APPLYING THE STANDARDS TO CASES

HOW TO USE PART II

The five standards for evaluating the ethical quality of police work that
we have developed in the first part of this book are of practical as well
as theoretical interest. The standards' theoretical interest is grounded
in the connections they make to a broader social contract perspective
on American values. The standards remind us that the moral principles
governing good police work are rooted in our notions of constitutional
government. The practical interest in these standards, on the other hand,
lies in our ability to apply them to concrete examples of the kinds of
situations police typically face and to use them to provide guidance
about how to handle those situations. If the standards are too general
to help the reader rank the merit of competing options that police must
consider in a situation, or if they are too specific to apply to the wide
range of situations police face in their work, then they will be of little
practical use. In order to establish the practical value of these standards,
it will be important to apply them to morally complex, yet typical cases
in order to demonstrate that they do illuminate these situations and
indicate preferred courses of action. That is the primary task of the
second half of this book.

In Chapters 4 through 7 we present and analyze a range of cases
through the lens of the five standards. Each scenario represents what
we called in the previous paragraph a ''morally complex, yet typical''
policing situation. We have selected these scenarios from among many
we have explored in classroom settings with police officers holding

virtually every possible rank, and from all regions of the country. The scenarios cover a range of circumstances common to police work: use of force, arrest, crowd control, dispute resolution and traffic regulation. The cases also touch on persistent dilemmas: whether and how to cooperate with colleagues, how to balance the rights of the public with the demands of loyalty to fellow officers and how to take risks on behalf of others while protecting oneself.

Following each scenario is a list of options that represent possible ways to respond to the scenario. Readers are invited to think of themselves (if they are not already) as police officers and should respond as if they were required (as officers often are) to choose a course of action from among the options. Try to think like a cop—that is, make a decision, do not take too long making it and second-guess yourself afterward.

We have selected the options not because they are perfect responses to the situation in the scenario, or even because they are highly creative. Rather, the options reflect a representative range of the kinds of actions that thoughtful officers have indicated they might take in such a situation if they faced it in real life. Some options are clearly preferable to others, but we in no way mean to imply that there is one and only one way to do police work. Although our discussion of each option will indicate what we think is clearly right and clearly wrong, most of the options fall into a "grey area" or into more ambiguous categories, such as "better" or "less preferable." Sometimes, options represent the difference between mere fulfillment of minimal duty and an attempt to excel.

The remainder of each chapter explores each option, and assesses its strengths and weaknesses as a response to the dilemmas posed by the scenario. During this phase of the analysis, we sometimes change the scenarios slightly to illuminate further the competing values and principles buried within them.

Our goal for Part II is to illustrate a pattern of reasoning, based on the use of the five standards elaborated in Part I, that allows a consistent and objective moral assessment of police action. Of course, readers familiar with examples of police conduct or decision-making other than those in Chapters 4 through 7 can apply the standards to those instances as well.

4

Rock Concert

The fundamental circumstances that make police work so systematically open to moral evaluation are the twin requirements of power and restraint. Police are both the bearers and symbols of power in our society. They are authorized to use coercive power in the maintenance of order and the enforcement of law, but because ours is a limited government, they must use that power with restraint. This regular combination of strength and limitation on strength can be confusing to the police and the public alike, and officers' confusion can be compounded by their need to rely on fellow officers for mutual support and protection when struggling with those who use force against them. Thus, dealings with colleagues in the context of exercising authority and power can also have significant moral implications. On occasion, the moral claims of the public and the moral claims of fellow officers intertwine with great complexity. Consider the following example:

You are one of a group of thirty officers from several different departments hired by the promoter to work in uniform at an indoor rock concert. You hold the rank of patrol officer. You have been assigned a supervisory sergeant, but he is from a department in a neighboring town. The groups performing are heavy metal and punk rock musicians. The crowd of 7,000 is composed mostly of teenagers.

Two acts have finished performing, and there are two more to go. The crowd is noisy but peaceable. The loudest element has been a group of fifteen to twenty leather-clad "Devil's Advocates," members of a motorcycle gang who have congregated on the auditorium floor a few rows from center stage. An officer from another town approaches you and tells you that he has observed a number of the cyclists apparently using cocaine and selling it to youthful members of the audience. He wants to arrest the cyclists who are dealing, and he asks you to accompany him.

Your previous experience with the Advocates tells you they often carry knives and even guns, and that it is a matter of honor for them to fight any police officer who tries to arrest them. You have also had experiences in which concert crowds have become violent as a result of police attempts to make drug or alcohol arrests.

Your fellow officer tells you that, whether you accompany him or not, he is going to make an arrest after the next band number begins.

As an officer in this situation, you cannot ignore your colleague's request for assistance or the safety of concert-goers. You must act or have a good justification for consciously refusing to act. Either way, you will have made a choice that has moral ramifications, a choice for which you may be judged—like it or not. Although there are many actions an officer might take in this situation, here are five courses of action that have been suggested by working police officers:

OPTION A: Accompany your fellow officer, and help him make the arrests.

OPTION B: Tell him you think the idea is dangerous, and advise him not to attempt the arrests. Accompany him if he insists on making the arrests.

OPTION C: Tell him you think the idea is dangerous, and advise him not to attempt the arrests. Decline to accompany him if he goes ahead anyway.

OPTION D: Contact your supervisor on your radio. Ask for backup help from other officers at the concert. Urge your colleague to wait until help arrives. When it does, make the arrests.

OPTION E. Advise the officer to observe the group, and identify those Devil's Advocates selling or in possession of cocaine. Call for backup and, working with a supervisor, plan to make arrests after the concert is over.

Surveying your choice of actions, as we have just done, should be the first step in any effort to arrive at a decision about what to do in a difficult situation. There is, of course, no fixed limit to this list, and the reader may have thought of a solution superior to any of the ones offered here. For illustrative purposes, the five offered above basically cover the ground in this case.

After surveying the options, it is useful to consider briefly which of the five standards of ethical police conduct are operative—or potentially operative—in this scenario. This will help us to organize our moral reasoning about how an officer should respond to the case. As you will see, the "rock concert" example involves elements of all five standards.

Although *fair access* is not the central element of this example, it must be considered in our deliberations. If you delay in taking immediate action against the Devil's Advocates, you must be sure that, by doing so, you are not denying police services to a group of concert-goers that needs them (e.g., those buying cocaine who may be harmed by using it or others in the audience who might be assaulted by a person under the cocaine's influence). Even those breaking the law may be entitled to your protection from the consequences of their own actions.

Public trust presents a more direct set of considerations in this example. Although no "abuse of office" elements arise here, your refusal to assist your fellow officer may represent a dereliction of your duty to enforce the law. Many members of the general public count on the police to enforce the drug laws vigorously, and a decision not to do so at least raises the question of whether you lack the courage and fortitude to uphold the public trust. Of course, refraining from a fight with a motorcycle gang in a crowded auditorium may, in fact, be a way to uphold the public trust.

This latter thought makes it clear that *safety and security* is a major, perhaps the central, focus of this example. That your colleague's action could set off a large-scale melee in a crowd of 7,000 must be taken seriously. Although the enforcement of drug laws is doubtless a priority for you and your department, the protection of the concert-goers, most of whom are innocent bystanders not involved in the purchase and sale of cocaine, cannot be of lesser concern. There are, in effect, two public safety issues here: protection of citizens from physical injury caused by (potentially avoidable or delayable) violence, and protection of citizens from the sale and use of illegal drugs occurring in your presence. What is not clear is whether both of these goals can be accomplished simultaneously.

Teamwork is another main focus of this example. Your colleague has made a direct request for help, and you are put in a position where responding affirmatively may go against your better judgment. Even if you feel that you have greater obligations to yourself, your family, your department or the public, the importance of loyalty to your fellow officer cannot be minimized. You may have concluded that your colleague has made a bad judgment in wanting to make an immediate arrest. In the police culture, however, the fact that a colleague asked for your help carries expectations of compliance and puts pressure on you to back him up.

Finally, there is the issue of *objectivity*. This standard requires you to be sure that your decision to support or decline your colleague's request is based on something other than personal prejudices or emotions. If you decline to back him up, for example, your unwillingness to take a risk cannot simply be based on your feeling that heavy metal rockers and young people "get what they deserve when they screw around with cocaine," no matter how "right" the decision against intervening might be from a tactical point of view. If, on the other hand, your willingness to help him arrest the Devil's Advocates stems from some hatred of them you acquired in some earlier incident, your judgment about the merits of intervening in this situation lacks the required objectivity.

Having placed your possible actions in the context of the five standards, we now turn to a careful discussion of each option to see which ones come closest to fulfilling your obligations under the standards. More precisely, in evaluating Options A through E, we should seek to eliminate any that might be an unacceptable violation of the standards. Then, among those options remaining, we want to decide which are simply adequate and which might be regarded as more desirable from the moral point of view. As we have noted, judging moral actions is not simply a matter of distinguishing good from bad. In the realm of the good, there is also better and best. This range of judgments falls along a continuum that Lon Fuller has called "the morality of duty" and "the morality of aspiration."[1]

The morality of duty defines a moral threshold below which actions are to be condemned. Meeting the threshold standard is a matter of doing one's duty, but such an action may be minimally praiseworthy. Within the realm of the acceptable, it is possible to meet a moral standard with varying degrees of value. An officer may "aspire" to a solution that promotes all the virtues of police excellence or may "get by" with an uninspired solution to the problem confronting him. This is not to say that every moral problem has a single "best" solution—or even that it has an acceptable solution. Nevertheless, every option open to an officer in such situations is subject to evaluation in light of the five moral standards, and can be assessed as inadequate, acceptable or better (that is, "beyond the call of duty"). Let us consider Options A through E according to this classification.

OPTION A: *Accompany your fellow officer and help him make the arrests.*

The first option, accompanying your fellow officer and helping him make the arrests, gives high priority to the requirements of *teamwork*. This standard obliges a police officer to cooperate, communicate and coordinate with fellow officers and other officials of the criminal justice system. One might argue, of course, that your colleague was not paying equal attention to teamwork when he told you that, whether you helped or not, he would make the arrest. However, at this point, we are trying to determine what your actions should be in response to your colleague's. His assertions are, first, a fact to take into account and then a behavior to evaluate. Because you can only be held accountable for what you do, it is of little use to wish he had presented the problem in a different form.

How does the standard of *teamwork* apply here? Law enforcement is often done most effectively as a collaborative activity. Drug raids, investigations, stakeouts, decoy operations and so forth are rarely if ever successful (or safe) if performed by a lone officer. Surely at this rock concert, and with suspects such as the Devil's Advocates, it would be futile for a lone officer to attempt to enforce the laws against drug dealing by himself. Assuming that both of you are experienced, competent and able to communicate, the two of you working collaboratively are much more likely to be effective than if either of you undertook to arrest a group of Advocates alone.

Beyond considerations of effectiveness are those of loyalty and mutual trust. Teamwork implies that individuals feel some bond and trust, as well as common purpose, among them. They must feel an obligation to offer aid and support to team members, and have confidence that their teammates will offer it in return.

Police work is more dangerous and stressful than most other occupations or professions. Generally speaking, occupations with measurable levels of risk or danger seem to generate higher levels of group solidarity or, more precisely, the expectation that colleagues will be ready to back up each other. Bench-clearing brawls in team sports are an example of this tendency. In the scenario under consideration here, where your "teammate" is willing to confront a group of predictably resistant individuals who are flagrantly violating the law, he doubtless expects that you, a fellow officer, will meet the requirements of *teamwork* as he defines them.

Accompanying your colleague to make the arrests can also be said to meet the requirements of *public trust*, since the public depends upon the police to protect it from dangerous individuals who commit crimes. By arresting those Devil's Advocates who were dealing drugs, the police can meet their obligation to protect society from criminal activity and the dangers of drug use.

Although making the arrest appears to meet two standards of ethical police work (*teamwork* and *public trust*), it also seems to pose a serious challenge to *safety and security*. This standard enjoins police officers to balance the obligations of law enforcement with the necessity to protect public safety. For two officers to attempt to arrest even one Advocate on the crowded floor of a rock concert might set off a melee that could endanger spectators more immediately and more seriously than the sale or use of cocaine. Experienced police officers say that at rock concerts there are few guarantees that members of the audience will act rationally, particularly if they have been using drugs or drinking alcoholic beverages. Another problem is that the Devil's Advocates may be armed, possibly with guns. Your decision to intervene must take account of some probability that they have weapons and are prepared to use them. It would be risky enough to approach them after the concert with fewer bystanders around; to approach them in mid-concert on the floor of the auditorium with 1,000 or more persons in the immediate vicinity would place those bystanders, regardless of their involvement with the drugs or their attitude toward the police, at a potentially avoidable risk of injury. Should the Devil's Advocates cause such injuries, of course, they would be directly responsible, but should a bystander be injured because of your decision to intervene when that intervention was avoidable or capable of being made in some other way, you would share some responsibility for precipitating injury to persons not directly involved in the crime. Although raising the possibility of gun play makes this example very dramatic, the essential point remains the same. Even if we were to imagine that an arrest attempt led to a fight without weapons between the Advocates and yourselves, bystanders might still be hurt and, to the degree that your ends could have been achieved in some other, less drastic way, you would still be indirectly responsible for avoidable harm.

In many jurisdictions, police departments have adopted policies that prohibit a police officer from firing a weapon at a suspect if the shots might strike innocent bystanders—even if this self-imposed restraint on the use of deadly force means letting a dangerous suspect escape. This is a cost/benefit judgment the officer's department makes when adopting such a policy. In the department's judgment, the cost involved in harming bystanders is greater, on balance, than the benefit involved in capturing suspects. Although it would be best to both capture the suspect and protect the general populace, where both goals cannot be achieved, departments opt for the result they consider paramount: avoiding injury to innocent bystanders. In this scenario, it seems appropriate to apply a similar standard: the sale of cocaine by the Devil's Advocates seems less of a threat than the possibility that a struggle with them might injure innocent members of the audience. Under the *safety and security* standard, even letting the Devil's Advocates go free seems preferable to harming the innocent.

Another possibility is that, innocent or not, nearby spectators might join with the Devil's Advocates in any fight against the police. This may be particularly true of those individuals who have been buying or using the Devil's Advocates' cocaine, but sometimes members of a crowd do things they would not normally do at other, less excitable moments. In other words, your arresting the Devil's Advocates may induce those whose better judgment is impaired by the effects of the drug and the environment of a heavy metal rock concert to oppose your efforts. To the degree that as a police officer you harm any of this category of participants, however much at that moment you might think of them as lawbreakers and deserving of punishment, you have at least partially contributed to this outcome.

Consider another variation. Suppose you decided to make the arrest, but are then overwhelmed by resistance. You might feel some obligation not to place innocent bystanders at risk and thus face two unpleasant choices: retreat without accomplishing your goal or absorb a beating. Retreating may involve a loss of face, but no immediate injury to yourself or others. To take a beating, on the other hand, rather than draw your weapon for fear of harming the innocent (if your instincts would allow such a thing) may be noble, but risks serious personal injury and pain, or even death.[2] From the point of view of duty and your obligation to provide *fair access* to your services, you must also weigh whether, if you are injured attempting to make the arrests, you will be available to provide safety for members of the public (for example, to offer first aid to a member of the audience who becomes ill) or to other officers who might, at some other part of the auditorium, require your assistance. You may, thinking in the longer term or broader social perspective, even argue that your injury or death would deprive your family, your department and your community of a valuable resource in which it had invested, and on whose availability it depends.

Consideration of the competing obligations of police officers reminds us that they must sometimes weigh the benefit of the services they choose to perform at the current moment against those they might be called upon to deliver in the relatively immediate future, say the next radio dispatch, or what they may find as they drive their patrol cars another mile down the road. They must always decide whether it is appropriate to become involved in a current situation (say, stop a motorist who committed a minor violation in their presence) or continue to patrol to look for more serious violations (say, to spot signs that a commercial premises may have been broken into). Put another way, one of the ways police must think of themselves is as a limited public resource whose efforts must be allocated on the basis of prioritized need and value.[3]

Thus, your colleague's request that you help him arrest the Devil's Advocates has to be evaluated as an appropriate investment of police resources at the concert. What must be balanced here is the risk of injury to yourself and others from a possible fight, the risk of injury to others due to cocaine distribution and use, and the preservation of police resources to do other kinds of tasks at the concert should they prove even more urgent than preventing the sale and use of drugs. Most officers we have worked with, when asked to identify their most pressing concern in this scenario, cited the dangers to innocents posed by a possible brawl as the most serious. These command greater attention than the potential harm done by the sale and use of drugs. As long as it is likely that the sale of drugs is less likely to prove dangerous to those present than the possibility of a brawl, *safety and security* requires that you not attempt to make an arrest.

Some police officers discussing this scenario have suggested that arresting the Devil's Advocates can be justified if there is a reasonable chance that two officers, acting alone, might be able to succeed without causing a brawl—even if that attempt entailed injury or risk to themselves. They argue that anything that could happen as a result of the arrest is no more dangerous to the crowd than the use of cocaine. They point out that officers can almost always justify inaction by saying they are saving themselves for something more serious than what is going on at present. If officers get too involved in the "big picture," they may never choose to get involved in the little things that make life so unpleasant for victims and those who suffer the incivilities of others' bad behaviors.

Granted, officers who define virtually all problems as "not big enough to be worth getting involved in" violate their obligation to take risks on behalf of others. Muir[4] would call such officers "avoiders." The issue, however, is one of degree. If the offense in question is not a clear and immediate threat to life and safety, if the probability of harm to bystanders is great if the officers intervene and if the context is such that other pressing demands for service are easy to anticipate, then officers must think of themselves as a scarce resource that might better be used attending to other matters. In this scenario, since the officers are likely to injure themselves and others if they intervene, and the harm done by the sale of cocaine is likely to be less than the injury created by a brawl, there seems little justification for intervention. *Option A*, in other words, *seems not to be acceptable*.

OPTION B: *Tell him you think the idea is dangerous and advise him not to attempt the arrests. Accompany him if he insists on making the arrests.*

This option is a more thoughtful application of the *teamwork* standard, because it makes some concessions to *safety and security*. Your actions would strike a compromise between trying to prevent an altercation and backing up your fellow officer. Given the discussion in the previous section, it is best to convince the other officer of the relative imprudence and predictable dangers to innocents of trying to intervene by yourselves. However, should your efforts to convince him fail, by backing him up you may meet the demands of *teamwork*.

Of course, all the objections we had to accompanying the officer in Option A still apply once he decides to undertake the arrest. It is hard to see how attempting to talk the officer out of an excessively dangerous situation justifies your subsequent participation in it (after all, you cannot justify your participation in a bank robbery by saying you tried to talk your compatriots out of it before pulling on your ski mask and handing the teller a note). Some officers have argued that, if a fellow officer makes a move to arrest suspects, no matter how ill-advised, they would feel obliged to join him—despite the obvious risks. They feel that contradicting him publicly, much less letting him take a beating, is disloyal and not self-respecting. Another way to think of this is to see the practice of backing up fellow officers as analogous to a group insurance policy: unless everyone pays the premium, none can be certain that the policy will pay dividends when it is cashed. Put another way: if an officer chooses not to back up a colleague because he considers doing so ill-advised or dangerous, then others are free not to back him up when he undertakes a risk. Seeing this as the case, no one will any longer take risks, and the public will find their police unreliable.

Although we sympathize with officers who feel obligated to back up a fellow officer in vulnerable circumstances (even if that officer put himself at risk as the result of impulsiveness, subjectivity or incompetence), those who accompany the officer in this scenario must bear responsibility for any avoidable injuries they may inflict on the innocent. Thus, the apparently more thoughtful response to *teamwork* proposed in Option B cannot outweigh the importance of *safety and security*. This shows that living up to some standards as fully as possible is still inadequate if a more important standard is ultimately sacrificed. *Option B is*, on these grounds, *unacceptable*.

> OPTION C: *Tell him you think the idea is dangerous and advise him not to attempt the arrests. Decline to accompany him if he goes ahead.*

Our experience is that, by itself, this is a difficult option for many police officers to select, but one that some of the most experienced officers in our discussions selected as a proper and defensible choice. When this option is presented to recruits in preservice training, however, almost none see this choice as acceptable.

We think the difference between the two categories of participants can be accounted for by the fact that most recruits have a somewhat exaggerated notion of the imperatives of loyalty and solidarity among police officers, whereas older officers tend to be more self-protective and less willing, at least in classroom discussion, to take risks on behalf of "hotdogging" fellow officers. On the street, as opposed to the classroom, we think it relatively rare, although not unheard of, for an officer to decline to back up another officer in trouble (many of us carry in our mind's eye the Hollywood image of wounded officer Frank Serpico left to die by his angry comrades, but this case, if true, is the rarest of exceptions). By contrast, officers are legendary for their willingness to respond to a dispatch indicating "officer down" or "officer needs assistance." When a fellow officer is shot or killed, many members of most departments will volunteer to work long hours until the murderer is apprehended.

There is more than romantic loyalty involved in this relentless search for "cop killers." In part, it is meant as a deterrent to attacks on the police; any civilian who kills an officer must know that his or her colleagues will not rest until the offender comes to justice. In part, this attitude is the result of conditioning: academy training, department ceremonies and locker room talk are all designed to promote solidarity (even though this attitude can spill over into a "them against us" mentality that undercuts police restraint toward certain segments of the public). Partly this loyalty arises as the natural outcome of working closely with others under conditions of stress or danger; some officers report that they feel closer to their partners than they do to their spouses.

Yet there are limits to the requirements of group loyalty. One is when the act of solidarity would entail, in the eyes of the officer whose loyalty is being called on, unacceptable or excessive personal risk. Some officers argue that their highest obligation is to themselves, in other words, to survival; they sometimes express this obligation as one they owe their spouses and children to "come home at night." The obligation to stay alive outweighs the obligation to support a colleague who has botched an assignment or who uses needlessly dangerous tactics when safer alternatives are available. Some of those who declined to support the officer in the scenario qualified their remarks by observing that he was from another department, not a regular partner or that the work was a private detail and not a regular street assignment. This is not to say that police will not take extreme risks for colleagues, whether partner or stranger, when no alternative exists.

Police recruits, perhaps because they tend to be young and thus less often married or parents, are less cognizant of the competing obligations among self, family, colleagues, departmental regulations, demands of the police culture and public expectations. Nor are they experienced at prioritizing the competing pulls of each. Recruits are also less likely than experienced officers to concede that they might not take on a particular law enforcement task just because it seemed risky. One senses that many officers (at all levels of experience) are reluctant to admit that they might not back up a colleague because they felt the risk to themselves too great. Perhaps the fear of not sounding courageous (or because such expressions of truthfulness seem outside the police culture's norms as the recruits know it) compels the fledgling officers to profess unqualified loyalty to fellow officers.

The risks of police work may require that officers overlook some of its most obvious elements. Skolnick[5] reminds us that danger is an omnipresent element in police work that helps shape the officer's "working personality." Although suspiciousness is an ever-present attitude among most police officers Skolnick and others have studied, we suspect that too much consciousness of fear could make the police officers' job intolerable or lead officers to acts of cowardice that would lower their self-esteem. Being somewhat "mindless" to danger and fear, then, might be a good strategy for maintaining job satisfaction.[6] A psychologist might define this form of thinking as "denial."

To test whether concerns for self or innocent bystanders really are more compelling than the necessity to back up a fellow officer, we have occasionally asked the participants whether they feel obligated to restrain their colleague physically should he insist on moving against the Devil's Advocates. Some participants have claimed that they would indeed try to hold their fellow officer back, either on the grounds of his safety or to prevent a riot. Others find this excessive: some because they think it bad for the public to see officers openly disagree, others because they do not believe in interfering in the performance of colleagues to that degree and yet others because they would withdraw their own objections and doubts if a fellow officer felt so certain about taking action where a clear violation of law existed. Clearly, the idea of laying hands on a colleague is a *very* controversial step.

In our view, if ethical police work requires the two of you to refrain from arresting the Devil's Advocates during the concert, then you should exert yourself to prevent your colleague from making this tactical error. The exertions must not put you or others at greater risk than the arrest (you are not required to succeed at any cost), but to the degree that they are less risky than the actions contemplated by the officer you are restraining, it is your obligation to act to restrain him. However impractical or uncomfortable this act may be (and only a handful in any group have insisted they would take it), *safety and security* can be construed to require you to restrain your colleague.

Although thus far we have explored a number of competing obligations that officers must reconcile, we have not yet addressed the question of whether it is permissible for police officers to choose *not* to act against a suspect when they have clear probable cause to believe that a felony had been committed. Whether or not a fellow officer has asked you to act, you may have an obligation at least to attempt to arrest individuals who engage in serious felonies, such as selling cocaine, despite the fact that there are risks to self and others involved. If an officer has an obligation to enforce the law, it is only heightened when he or she is asked to do so by a fellow officer. Put another way, do officers really have discretion to overlook crimes considered as serious as the sale of cocaine at a public event?

This question is, in effect, a challenge to the very logic of *safety and security*. It asserts that law enforcement is not so much a means to public order but an end in itself. Indeed, it asserts that enforcement of the law is an unqualified obligation for officers who are witness to a violation. Police officers are well aware, in a way that most of us are not, that they are normally granted a wide discretion in choosing when and how to carry out their duties. Most laws, even those against possession or sale of dangerous narcotics, specify that a police officer may (as opposed to shall) arrest upon probable cause to believe the law has been violated. Rarely does the law prescribe the details of officers' actions;[7] they are allowed a wide latitude to choose when and how to respond to a violation of law. They may not consider the crime serious enough to merit action (for example, jaywalking or minor traffic infractions), they may consider action premature (allowing a criminal to commit a series of acts in order to build a stronger case against him for trial) or they may find other priorities more compelling (overlooking a minor drug sale in front of premises that are the subject of an undercover stakeout).

Put another way, police officers have no iron-clad, inflexible legal obligation to make arrests whenever they see a law violated. When the officer who witnesses a violation does not make an arrest, we may have the urge to make an initial presumption of neglect, corruption, laziness or cowardice, but there are literally innumerable good reasons for failing to arrest. Safety is surely one such reason. Where officers have discretion not to arrest for good and valid reasons, they have the discretion not to act even if requested to do so by a fellow officer. (Of course, they may have an obligation to do so if legally ordered by a superior officer.) In this instance, the discretion not to act is reinforced by the ethical obligations of *safety and security*. Option C seems to uphold *safety and security* without violating any other standards and thus represents an ethically acceptable course of action, even if it violates many officers' notions of the imperatives of the police culture.

> **OPTION D:** *Contact your supervisor on your radio. Ask for backup help from other officers at the concert. Urge your colleague to wait until help arrives. When it does, make the arrests.*

This option has several virtues. It meets the obligation to avoid the unacceptable risks entailed in a solo or two-person arrest attempt. It gathers a group of officers together, which holds the promise of discouraging resistance from the Devil's Advocates. It also provides you and others in the crowd with a much better protection should they resist. In other words, calling for backup draws on the best aspects of police teamwork and solidarity.

It does not, however, answer the general question about the wisdom of attempting to arrest Devil's Advocates during the concert itself. Partly, this answer can only be given in the specific circumstances of a real-life event. In actual police work, an officer will subjectively (that is, intuitively) assess the mood of the crowd, the likelihood of any members of the audience taking the Devil's Advocates' side, whether or not violence had previously occurred at the concert, how long the concert had been on, how crowded the auditorium was, how much alcohol or drug consumption had been allowed, how close the Devil's Advocates were to the exits and thus how long it might take to remove them from the auditorium and myriad other factors that go into a police officer's calculations. The fact that the officers working the concert were not from a single department, and thus not trained to act as a unit, would also diminish the likelihood of their being able to control the melee if the Devil's Advocates resisted arrest.

However, our task is not to assess the wisdom of an arrest attempt from a tactical perspective; rather, it is to raise moral considerations about the various potential consequences of the attempt—to weigh the cost of possible failure in its various forms against the value of its success. One way to get at the proportionality between risks and ends is to ask whether you would assist your colleague in his attempt to arrest the drug dealers were they "preppie" college students or young, middle-class professionals attending, say, a folk music festival rather than Devil's Advocates attending a heavy metal concert. Put another way, the question is whether it is preferable to forgo arresting *anyone* selling cocaine during a concert, or is it only preferable to do so if the sellers are reputedly dangerous individuals, such as Devil's Advocates or others who may potentially be carrying dangerous weapons and are notorious "cop fighters."

Altering the scenario to make the drug dealers non-threatening "preppie" college students and the setting a folk music festival increased the number of police participants who said they would join their colleague in making arrests, particularly after calling for backup. This group usually included even those who would have forgone the arrest (even with backup) if the sellers were Devil's Advocates. When asked why they would have been willing to arrest "preppies," some participants offered their belief that cocaine selling *is* a very serious offense, and that cocaine use could be unpredictably and suddenly dangerous to its users. Since the "preppies" were unlikely to offer significant resistance or pose a threat to others, and their drug sales posed a threat to the buyers, they should have been arrested. When the participants were asked if they would make arrests if the sales were of marijuana, some of those willing to arrest for cocaine declined. This would indicate that it was the harmfulness of cocaine and not the selling of drugs per se that was morally relevant to them. Others would arrest any drug dealer if the arrest could be effected safely, regardless of the drug being sold.

Yet a minority of officers held out against arrest even of presumptively "unthreatening" college students or young professionals, and precisely on the grounds of personal and bystander safety. They point out that drugs have a reality-distorting capacity, and cocaine in particular has a tendency to delude its users into a false sense of powerfulness. Even normally meek individuals under cocaine's influence, suddenly faced with the prospect of arrest, might overestimate their capacity to resist the police. Also, although a hard-core group of drug sellers would be unlikely to have many sympathizers in a folk festival, the arrest of "one of their own" at the folk festival might set off waves of protest even in a middle-class adult audience and a riot might ensue. In short, these officers still see an arrest as an unnecessary risk, regardless of the

characteristics of the actors involved. They also see police interaction
with those under the influence of drugs as inherently less predictable
than interactions with those same individuals when sober. *We tend to
agree, and find that Option D, although wiser than the others, is still
defective.*

OPTION E: *Advise the officer to observe the Devil's Advocates, and
identify those selling or in possession of cocaine. Call for backup and,
working with a supervisor, plan to make arrests after the concert is over.*

This option seems to offer the best balance between upholding the
law and maximizing public safety. Identifying the dealers and observing
them outside the auditorium in possession of at least some of what they
were selling would suffice for probable cause to arrest them. Waiting
until the Devil's Advocates were outside the auditorium lowers the risk
to you that other concert-goers will come to their aid and certainly
lowers the risk of injury to other concert-goers. This action meets the
standards of *public trust, safety and security, and teamwork.*

By placing the offenders under arrest, you have met your public
obligation to uphold the law even at some risk to yourself (public trust).
By waiting until the Devil's Advocates were in a location in which a
confrontation would threaten fewer individuals, you have better accom-
modated the requirements of public safety (safety and security). By
assisting your fellow officers in making the arrest, and by encouraging
your fellow officers to follow a course of action less dangerous to
themselves, you have met the tests of teamwork. You were also willing
to observe and identify those individuals who were selling or in possession of the cocaine, rather than wade into the crowd and run the risk
of a mistaken arrest during the ensuing confusion. Thus, you have shown
the kind of careful police work needed to help a prosecutor earn a
conviction when you testify in court, and you have met the broader
requirement of teamwork that demands cooperation with other segments
of the criminal justice system. On balance, then, Option E seems to be
the best of those presented, since it meets three of the standards and
does not appear to violate the other two. Each of the previous options,
to some degree, violated *safety and security.*

It is nevertheless possible to raise some objections to Option E. There
is a clear health risk to the users in allowing them to take cocaine until
the concert is over. They may in fact consume or toss away all of the

remaining evidence, leaving you with a weaker case at the prosecutorial stage than if you had arrested them in possession of it. You may also feel that, by letting the Devil's Advocates use and sell cocaine in plain view during the concert, members of the audience might believe that you condone or tolerate its use. Thus, in some people's eyes, you might give the appearance of favoritism, a violation of *fair access*. Worse, if members of the crowd come to believe that the Devil's Advocates have extorted or purchased privileges and immunities from law enforcement that others in society do not have, they may believe you have violated your public trust. After all, the great majority of concert-goers will not see you make an arrest after the crowd has cleared out.

These objections address issues regarding the image as well as the content of your choice, on ethical grounds, to refrain from arresting the Devil's Advocates during the concert. The public's misapprehension of your attitude or tolerance toward Devil's Advocates or drug dealing seems insignificant compared to their likely reaction should your precipitate actions spark a riot or a death. As most police officers know, there are a limited number of things that the police can do to create a positive attitude toward themselves among audiences attending heavy metal concerts, or to convince the general public in any context that they are always fair and even-handed, or have good cause not to enforce obvious violations of the law. Police work is unlikely to win public understanding or tolerance on the basis of one particular incident.

However, police work done consistently well over time, that is, police work that lives up over the years to the five ethical standards, will, in the long run, win approval from the great majority of the public. Even where ethical police performance is unpopular (say, among those who would prefer to break the law or who enjoy violating the rights of others), it is nonetheless imperative that police meet the ethical standards of their profession and not simply seek public acceptance or appreciation of their efforts. After all, it has been in periods when the police tolerated popular but illegal activities, such as lynchings and bootlegging, that public confidence in their honesty and integrity was at an all-time low.[8] Where ethics competes with popularity, ethics must win out.

NOTES

1. Lon L. Fuller, *The Morality of Law*, revised ed. (New Haven: Yale University Press, 1969), pp. 5–32.

2. We have heard stories of officers who have absorbed beatings rather than draw weapons that would place others at unnecessary risk, although we think such acts require enormous self-discipline. One training academy director has told us that he tells his recruits, "If you aren't willing to take a beating, don't get into police work. There will come a time when someone bigger and stronger will whip you, and you'll just have to take it." A state trooper who worked the isolated villages of northern Alaska told us that his rule was, "If you aren't prepared to take a suspect in a fist fight, don't threaten to arrest him with a gun. You're too isolated, and there's no one to back you up. If you're armed and he's not, one of his friends might shoot you and claim self-defense. If you whip him in a fair fight, he'll respect you and come along without trying to escape. If you take him at gun point, he'll feel he can get the drop on you later."

3. In *Police: Streetcorner Politicians* (Chicago: University of Chicago Press, 1977), pp. 95–97, William Ker Muir, Jr., discussed the dilemma posed by Officer Tom Hooker, who was skilled at mediating family arguments, but who spent as much as an hour or two calming the participants, analyzing the problems they presented and counseling them on solutions. In terms of the five standards of ethical police work, Hooker's approach poses a fair-access issue. By spending that much time applying his clinical skills to arguments, his other constituents may have been denied access to his other services (for example, his time spent in random patrol). Although counseling may have been a good use of Hooker's talents, it may have been offered to a small handful of all those he was obligated to serve, and at the cost of his providing a wider range of services to all who were eligible to receive them.

4. Ibid., pp. 55–57.

5. Skolnick suggests that a police officer's "working personality" is developed as a defense against the threats to harm that constantly lurk in his or her daily work. "Why Police Behave the Way They Do," in Jerome H. Skolnick and Thomas C. Gray, *Police in America* (Boston: Little, Brown, 1975), p. 31.

6. Muir refers to officers who pursue a "minimax" strategy of policing: they always approach members of the public in ways that minimize the maximum risk, that is, they approach them as if they were dangerous. The unpleasant side of this approach for the officer is that he or she begins to see all members of the public as hostile, feels isolated and then hated and finds that his or her job has no pleasant or relaxed moments in it—a job not worth having. *Police: Streetcorner Politicians*, p. 40.

7. In some states, domestic violence statutes prescribe the steps officers must take in addressing victims of domestic assault.

8. Perhaps the nadir of American policing was the 1920s, during the age of Prohibition, but through most of the nineteenth century as well as the 1920s, American police were considered corrupt extensions of local political machines. See Robert Fogelson, *Big-City Police* (Cambridge, Mass.: Harvard University Press, 1977), for a more thorough discussion of this point.

5

Dispute over a Bicycle

In the previous chapter, we considered a situation in which the potential for violence was great and the violations of law were obvious. Although police must be prepared for cases such as these, by most accounts they arise relatively infrequently in police work. Numerous studies have confirmed that most incidents involving the police are undramatic calls for service and assistance, or routine matters of law enforcement such as traffic stops. However, it would be a mistake to think that moral issues are limited only to the most difficult and dangerous aspects of police work. Even in their most routine, day-to-day dealings with the public, police officers make decisions, and take actions that have moral consequences and that can meet—or fail to meet—the five standards.

The following example asks you to analyze one of the most commonplace, yet most difficult, situations for a police officer to handle: a dispute in which there is not an obviously right or wrong party, and in which each party seeks "justice" from a police officer. In such a scene, officers have multiple concerns that sometimes compete with each other for priority: finding a satisfactory resolution to the argument, preventing escalation from verbal conflict to violence, forestalling future repetitions of the conflict and so forth. As you analyze the scenario that follows, try to ask yourself not only what you would do, but what goals you hope to accomplish by taking your chosen action.

You are a patrol officer riding alone in a patrol car on a warm October weekday afternoon at approximately 4:00 P.M. You receive a dispatch to handle a disturbance in a public playground.

When you arrive, a middle-aged white woman and a black youth are each tugging at the handlebars of a ten-speed bicycle and yelling at each other. A racially mixed group of about eight boys who appear to be ages eleven through thirteen surrounds the two disputants.

When you make your presence known to the group, the woman tells you that the bicycle belongs to her son. Her son told her two days ago that the bike was stolen from him at knife point by a black youth. She says this boy matches her son's description of his assailant, and she insists that you arrest the boy and allow her to take the bicycle home. She goes on to ask you why the police allow the playground to be occupied by black kids who are not from the neighborhood and complains that the police are no longer interested in keeping "good people" safe.

You ask the boy his version of the story. Looking as if he is about to cry, he tells you that he bought the bike for cash two days ago from a white boy who he had seen around the neighborhood, but whose name and address he does not know. He tells you he paid for the bike with funds he had saved from doing errands. The boy's companions, both black and white, support his story.

August Vollmer has observed that a patrol officer needs "the wisdom of Solomon, the patience of Job."[1] The patience of Job would surely be an asset in this instance, but a Solomonic proposal—such as offering to cut the bicycle in half—is unlikely to appeal to either contestant. What are a police officer's options? Here are a few that are commonly suggested:

OPTION A: Arrest the boy on suspicion of armed robbery, and give the woman the bicycle.

OPTION B: Tell the boy to remain at the playground with you and the bike; send the woman to get her sales receipt or registration, and bring her son back to identify the boy; investigate the case against the boy further if the woman produces proof or her son identifies him as the assailant.

OPTION C: Take the bicycle and bring it to the police station (leave the park); take each disputant's name and address, and those of the other boys; send the woman to get her sales receipt or registration. If the woman fails to produce proof, return the bike to the boy. If the woman produces proof, investigate the case against the boy further.

OPTION D: Take the bicycle to the station (leave the park); ask the disputants to bring proof or witnesses to their ownership; order the disputants to leave the playground.

OPTION E: Regardless of your other actions, reprimand the woman for her racial comments.

This example, like that in Chapter 4, raises a number of questions about how police officers are to live up to the five standards. Because minorities and juveniles are often treated with more suspicion than middle-class white adults by police and segments of the public, in this case you need to be attentive to the requirements of *fair access*. Initially, both parties to the dispute have a claim on your services, even though one of those claims is likely to be unjustified in the end. She is asking for a return of "her" property; he is asking for protection of property he swears he has purchased. You must resolve this property dispute or at least figure out a method for resolving it. *Public trust* is also a concern here because the parties are vulnerable to your coercion. This is particularly true of the black youth, who, realistically speaking, has difficult recourse if you take his bike, since he admits he has no bill of sale. If his rights and claims are protected in his confrontation with the woman, it will be because you are attentive to them. *Safety and security* may also be a concern in this scenario if you believe that the situation carries the potential for violence between the woman and the youths. The accusations are sufficiently serious and the tempers sufficiently short that the possibility of threats and harm is a real one should you depart. There are no obvious matters of *teamwork* in this example, unless you choose to refer the case to a court. Then, your presentation in a report or testimony in court would strongly shape the outcome of the case. How you wrote that report and testified, if necessary, would doubtless influence the judge's decision and, in a criminal case (if there was one), the prosecutor's charges as well. Finally, *objectivity* could become a question if the officer responds too strongly, or not strongly enough, to the racial dimension of the situation. Clearly, then, the moral dimensions of this situation are not trivial. An officer would need to weigh the various options in light of the ethical requirements of the job. Let us review each option in closer detail.

OPTION A: *Arrest the boy on suspicion of armed robbery, and give the woman the bicycle.*

The virtue of this approach lies in the possibility that the bicycle belongs to the woman's son, and then the further related likelihood that the black youth is either guilty of armed robbery or, at a minimum, receiving stolen property. Arresting the boy and booking him on suspicion of armed robbery may help make an entire neighborhood safer and assure that justice is done in this case (in the sense of initiating a process by which the guilty party may be adjudicated guilty and punished). Some officers suggest using your radio to call headquarters to see whether the woman had filed a stolen bicycle report two days ago. This would both raise her credibility and give you further grounds on which to take the boy into custody. However, since many individuals feel that filing reports of stolen property with the police is a waste of time unless the property is insured, her failure to file a report is not necessarily telling in this case.

However, the *fair-access* standard asserts that the police are a social resource and must provide their services on an equitable basis to all. As referees, the police must make judgments regarding when and how the rules of the game (the terms of the social contract) have been violated. However, those judgments must be made by criteria that apply equally to all players. At this point, the woman is claiming that the bicycle in question is her son's, but many bicycles look alike. She has not produced proof of ownership (a sales receipt, bicycle registration or other form of documentation). Nor has she produced any witnesses to the boy's involvement in a crime. The boy, on the other hand, has witnesses to support his claim that he bought the bike from another youth. There is no compelling reason to give her account more weight than his—to give her better access to the coercive authority that you as a police officer may use at your discretion in situations such as these. Conversely, of course, there is no compelling reason to believe his version of events either.

Generally, adults are inclined to take the word of other adults over that of juveniles (and often this is so for good reasons). White adults are even more likely to be inclined to accept the word of another white adult in preference to that of a black youth. However, police bear a special obligation under the *objectivity* standard to resist the temptation to identify with disputants or complainants who are most like themselves. In this case, two standards, *fair access* and *objectivity*, combine to establish that arresting the boy and giving the bike to the woman on the current evidence would be unacceptable.

OPTION B: *Tell the boy to remain at the playground with you and the bike; send the woman to get her sales receipt or registration, and bring her son back to identify the boy; investigate the case against the boy further if the woman produces proof or her son identifies him as the assailant.*

This choice has much to commend it. If the woman did purchase the bicycle for her son, she can stake her claim for its return by producing this tangible proof. If the boy was her son's assailant, the son can identify him, and you than have probable cause to arrest him. You can also search him for a knife, which if found will serve as corroborating evidence to implicate the boy. Should the scenario play itself out this way, you would take a potentially dangerous offender and his weapon out of circulation in the neighborhood. Without question, this series of steps holds out the promise of doing justice and improving neighborhood safety.

However, it might undermine some of the boy's legal rights, with implications for your living up to the ethical standards of good police work. For one thing, telling the boy he must wait with you in the playground until the woman's son arrives would deprive the boy of his liberty—it effectively places him under arrest. Thus far, a majority of our program participants have concluded that you do not appear to have probable cause (the legal threshold) to arrest him.

The legal standard of probable cause requires that there be a sufficient pattern of facts to warrant your actions. However, the boy has witnesses to support his claim of having bought the bike, whereas the woman who is accusing him of stealing it was not a witness to the crime, if indeed a crime occurred, and thus cannot accurately identify this boy as its perpetrator. If you hold him against his will without sufficient probable cause, you have violated *public trust*, which enjoins you not to use unnecessary or unauthorized coercion against members of the public. The boy has no safe way to resist your command or defy your authority. You are the police, armed and powerful, and he is just a twelve-year-old boy under your control. You must not overuse the power inherent in your authority, even if it would be an efficient way to bring this dispute to an end. Lacking probable cause to arrest, you cannot detain the boy for very long while the woman seeks out her son and brings him back to the playground.

Of course, when issues regarding an officer's legal authority to detain, search or arrest are at question, there is room for disagreement and debate. Some participants have concluded that, in this scenario, they do have sufficient probable cause to arrest, whereas others have argued that, given the allegation that the boy is an armed robber, they can at least "pat him down" to see if he has a knife. They claim the set of facts in the scenario might be interpreted as justifying a quick frisk on the grounds that, if the woman is correct, the boy represents a threat to her and to the officer. Should a knife be found, then placing the boy under arrest would be justified.

However, a majority of participants have found the case against the boy too circumstantial to justify even the minimal intrusion of a frisk. There are several Supreme Court decisions enumerating constitutional rights that imply a frisk in these circumstances would be illegal, above all because the woman cannot make an accurate identification of the boy as the likely suspect: she was not a witness to the crime. Unjustified searches are unnecessarily intrusive—as a free people, there is a sphere of privacy we are all entitled to expect and the police have to respect. We would argue that constitutional considerations in this instance co-incide with the *public trust* standard. Young citizens should not come to believe that the police can lay hands on them whenever adults decide they are "suspicious." Youths are entitled to the same respect as adults, unless they do something to squander it. Option B, then, is inadequate because it encourages you to overstep your authority.

OPTION C: *Take the bicycle and bring it to the police station (leave the park); take each disputant's name and address, and those of the other boys; send the woman to get her sales receipt or registration. If the woman fails to produce proof, return the bike to the boy. If the woman produces proof, investigate the case against the boy further.*

To many participants, this is the preferred, that is, most fair, of the possible solutions to this situation. Since the bicycle is the object of the dispute, you are holding it in trust for both sides. This action has the distinct virtue of moving the venue of the dispute from the park to the police station, effectively ending the public disturbance and sepa-rating the disputants. Removing the object of debate from the presence of the debaters enhances their *safety and security*, while allowing you time to sort through the legal issues in the matter.

You have also taken a major step toward establishing ownership of the bike. Many bicycles have a serial number that should appear on a bill of sale, so if the woman appears with a bill of sale for the bicycle, her original ownership should be easy to establish. Taking the boy's name allows you to release him (we just discussed why taking him into custody could be considered an unwarranted overextension of your authority). If she has a bill of sale, you can call the boy in for questioning, and her son can identify or exonerate him as the assailant. On the contrary, if the woman cannot produce a receipt, the bike can be returned to the boy.

Yet, there are certain pitfalls and inequities in this option. For one, it seems to lack even-handedness. The boy has already told you that he has no receipt for the bike, so he cannot produce his own conclusive proof of having purchased it for cash from another boy. He can only hope that the woman has no receipt or that the one she produces is not for his bike. Even if she produced a receipt it would not be proof that the boy stole the bike, rather than purchased it for cash, in good faith, from a third party.

It is possible, in other words, that both parties are telling the truth: the boy might have bought the bike for cash from a white youth, and it might well be her son's bike. One possibility is that the bike was stolen from her son at knife point by a black youth, and then bought, restolen by, or stolen on behalf of or in partnership with a white youth who then sold it for cash to the black youth now standing before you. Still, if this were the case, the boy would be guilty of having received stolen property, even if he did so unwittingly.

Let us complicate the legal issue of property ownership even more. One (possibly quite cynical) participant suggested to us that we could not dismiss the possibility that the woman's son actually sold the bike to the black youth and then told her a story about its being stolen at knife point so that she would buy him another. You might for this reason alone (thinking like a cynical cop) insist that the mother bring her son to the station so that the two boys might confront each other—of course, the officer would have to request or compel the black youth to appear at the station to identify and be identified by the woman's son. Again, this might be tantamount to placing the youth under arrest, or compelling him to incriminate himself by telling him he has to appear at the station when you have no probable cause to arrest him.

Some officers have suggested that, even without receipts, they would want the boy to come to the station and summon his parents to reclaim "his" bike for him. Their motive for taking the bike into custody was not so much to resolve a property dispute as to assure themselves that the youth's parents knew he had been accused of armed robbery. The officers wanted to know whether the parents would come to their boy's defense, whether they would indicate that the boy had a history of previous trouble and whether they would seem able to control their son. Partly, this would be to assure themselves that the boy would not retaliate against the woman or her son if the bike was taken from him, partly to determine if the boy's story was in any way credible and partly it would be a way of making a moral assessment of whether the boy was "a bad kid" or a "good kid" who deserved "a break" should there be a need to file charges of theft or receiving stolen property in juvenile court.

This option is difficult to implement, however. The woman has indicated that the youth is not from the neighborhood. Few eleven or twelve year olds carry identification. You might ask the boy his name and address, but if he is hardened enough to take the bike at knife point, he is probably clever enough to lie about his name and address. Although sending him home voluntarily for his parents might be the only choice permitted to you constitutionally (arguably, even this action might be excessively coercive, because the youth is unlikely to know you cannot lawfully order him to reappear at the station), it runs the risk of your letting a guilty party go free. Some officers have suggested driving the boy home so that you can find out where he lives and whether his parents corroborate his story. This, too, however, flirts with placing him unconstitutionally under arrest. In each community, public and departmental expectations may allow officers to take juveniles home in cases like these, but driving him home to corroborate suspicions may violate *public trust* because it may be excessively coercive to compel the boy to enter your patrol car, since he is not lost, disabled or under arrest.

Thus far, we have dealt with this incident primarily as a property dispute (a *fair-access* issue) and hedged in your responses by holding you to tightly limited exercise of your authority (compelled you through constitutional limitations to respect your *public trust*). Put another way, we have argued that the right of a police officer to use arrest as part of a solution to this scenario is limited by moral and constitutional constraints. What would happen if we changed our perspective and redefined the problem not as a property or constitutional law issue, but first and foremost as a public disturbance that could lead to personal injury to one or more parties? Let us see how this redefinition of priorities might change our choice of actions.

OPTION D: *Take the bicycle to the station (leave the park); ask the disputants to bring proof or witnesses to their ownership; order the disputants to leave the playground.*

As in the previous option, you have taken names and the bike, and asked people to bring proof of ownership to the station. What we have added here is your insistence that the disputants leave the park. In situations in which someone might get hurt, *fair access* and *safety and security* compel you to provide protection to the woman, the boy and all his friends. The injunction to keep everyone safe might mean that, as a police officer, you would feel a need to disperse the group of boys or make certain that the woman left the playground. After all, even if the argument stopped while you were present, both disputants might feel a need to remain at the playground simply to avoid the appearance of losing face after you left. Even if you confiscated the bike, the disputants might resume their argument. You might feel uneasy about leaving the woman alone in the park with eight or nine boys between the ages of eleven and thirteen, especially after she has issued racial remarks and accused one of their number of being a thief. Compelling the woman, the boys or both to leave the park is one way to assure yourself that, for now at least, they will not harm each other.

As with arresting the boy in Option B, you may not have sufficient legal grounds to compel anyone to leave the scene once the disputing has stopped. Some participants have argued that, since you were called to quell a disturbance in a public place, you can take any necessary measures to attain your mission, and compelling the disputants to depart falls within this range of permissible uses of police authority. Other experienced officers believe that such commands, once peace is restored, exceed your authority.

Perhaps the *safety and security* standard can shed some light on the limits to your authority in this instance. This standard asserts that police must balance maintaining safety of individuals and security of their property with the enforcement of laws and the upholding of constitutional rights. Usually, this standard is invoked to justify the use of police discretion to overlook violations of law when actions against violators would threaten some more important end or goal. For example, if making a traffic stop on a narrow, heavily traveled road during a rainy night would endanger an officer's safety or that of the offending driver, not stopping the violator even though he or she has broken the motor vehicle laws is justified.

However, *safety and security* can also be understood in its reverse formulation. We would argue that it may be necessary for police to assert their authority in the interests of *safety and security* even where the law provides no clear grounds to do so. We would want to limit police exercise of authority in such instances to ones in which the exercise is kept to its essential minimum, can be shown to address a clear (or clearly potential) threat to safety of individuals and its use is applied objectively and even-handedly. Within these criteria, politely ordering the woman, the boy or all the boys to leave the playground might, on ethical grounds, be justified even though the command could not survive constitutional scrutiny. It may be "smoother" or more acceptable to convince the parties to leave on some other ground (going home to get receipts, or to bring parents or witnesses to the station), but if you reasonably sense that leaving the disputants alone together after you leave could lead to more arguing, it would be negligent on your part to do so, even if you had to act somewhat coercively to get the parties to disperse for their own good.

As we have seen, Options C and D both seem to overstep the strictest limit of police authority in the interest of restoring order and solving the dispute. We would be surprised if police officers were not confronted by this trade-off with some regularity. In a sense, the goal of keeping order and the injunction to stay within the legal limits of police authority may at times be in conflict. Whether the use of legally unauthorized coercion is acceptable or not in this case will depend upon several things. In some communities, police are expected to establish order and, only then, refer to legal rights as a way to define techniques for doing so.[2] In others, the judgment of whether you could order the disputants to leave the park would be based on a widespread concern that the police "respect individual rights." Some departments set strict guidelines on the use of force and authority in cases like these, but for the most part, how your actions will be judged in this case is likely to be the product of whether the arguing, fighting or worse breaks out again after you leave the park.

OPTION E: *Regardless of your other actions, reprimand the woman for her racial comments.*

Some would argue that *fair access* requires you to address the woman's racially prejudiced remarks to the boys, who have a right not to be so abused. If the boys assaulted her for the remarks, they might have been seen as "fighting words," which would excuse the boys for using violence. Even if the boys took no offense at the woman's remarks, these participants point out, a police officer should be sensitive to the inappropriateness of her remarks, because the boys should not be allowed to think the police will let racist adults verbally abuse minorities. You might therefore want to tell the woman that minorities have the right to use the streets, to congregate in public places and to use peaceably all public facilities. You would be factually correct in telling her these things, and would be reaffirming for the boys that, even at their age, they are entitled to all the protections of citizenship granted to each individual under the terms of the social contract and the Constitution.

However, many officers (both black and white) suggest that there is no imperative to address her racial attitudes. For one thing, however unfortunate the fact, directing racial remarks at other people may be a constitutionally protected form of speech. Secondly, her lifelong bigoted opinions are unlikely to be affected by a lecture delivered by you, her "public servant." They note that such a lecture might heighten her anger or turn it against you instead of the boy. She might then escalate her remarks about the boy or blacks in general, forcing the officer to get into a "pissing contest" with her, perhaps ultimately having to place her in custody if she would not calm down or restrain her tongue. Even if the woman deserved such treatment, these officers argue, applying it would lead to a poor outcome in several respects. Ironically, you would end up having arrested someone who claims to be the mother of a crime victim. Furthermore, her remarks indicate that she is already alienated from the police, because you cannot or will not protect her and her son from dangerous "invaders" of her neighborhood. Your lecturing on minority rights will only convince her that you have taken the invaders' side, particularly if you happen to be a member of a minority yourself. There is also the possibility that she would file a complaint against you, and that you would have to justify your actions in written reports and at a hearing. Finally, if you provoked her into anger and an argument or worse, there would be the embarrassment of you, a fully armed police officer, having brought a middle-aged woman to the station in handcuffs for having "interfered with the duties of a police officer," much to the amusement of your professional peers.

Far easier than addressing her racist comments directly and risking these unpleasant consequences, many participants claim, it is best simply to keep her separated at some distance from the boys, and ask her politely but firmly to stick to the issue of bike ownership. This will protect the boys from her sharp tongue and keep the issue focused on successful identification of the bike's rightful owner. These officers suggest that, regardless of how benighted the woman's attitudes are, the dispute can only be made worse for all concerned by turning a property and safety issue into a racial issue. In sum, they find no ethical standard among the five that compels an officer to address the woman's racial attitudes or remarks other than to keep her apart from the boys while she remains riled.

Clearly, the schools of thought on how to handle the woman's remarks differ. Even experienced officers are unable, in our seminars, to agree on the proper course of action or on whether the woman has the right to speak her feelings. Our analysis of this typical, but far from simple, scenario has brought us to an understanding that there may be no ideal way to resolve a dispute or perform police work in general. You may have to struggle toward adherence to the five standards without completely satisfying them, but even where there is no ideal solution to a problem, there are those that are better and those that are worse. It remains your obligation to find the most acceptable course of action. Sometimes, it can be helpful to change some of the facts in the example. By doing this, we can identify those elements of the case that seem to carry the most moral significance for us and go back to the original version of the facts to assure ourselves that we have met our most important obligations in selecting from among our options.

Previously, we considered whether the incident at the playground should be seen as a stolen property issue, a debate on the limits of search and seizure, a public order/safety problem or a free speech issue. Let us now imagine that, after each side had presented its case to you but before you decided on a course of action, the woman suddenly began punching at the boy and pulling his hair, actually striking him once or twice and, although not hurting him seriously, scratching his face, making him let go of the bike and making him cry. Would these

new events change any of your ethical obligations as a police officer?
Would you be obliged to act differently? For example, would you have
to arrest the woman? What light do the five standards of police work
shed on this new situation?

In this new set of circumstances, you have clear evidence for the first
time—eyewitness evidence, at that—that a crime has been committed:
an assault and battery against the boy. Once again, let us review some
of your options in handling this violation of law in the context of the
dispute over the bicycle.

OPTION F: *Get the woman to relinquish her grip on the boy; separate
them; place her under arrest for assault and battery.*

Surely getting the woman to desist from hurting the boy and keeping
them separated are your first obligations as a police officer. This is the
absolute bare minimum of your responsibility and must be done before
any other action is taken. This is true regardless of who is right in the
case, whether the boy is innocent or, in fact, a bicycle thief. This would
be equally true if the reverse were the case, and he were assaulting the
woman in retaliation for her racial remarks. You would still be obliged
to restrain him even if you felt that she deserved her "punishment."
Under the terms of the social contract, the police are obliged and expected to restore and maintain order during private disputes or when
private assaults break out. If they do not, society has reverted to Locke's
"State of Nature" in which private citizens, not their agents (the police),
must use violence to regulate their own affairs and resolve their own
disputes.

Virtually all officers agree that you would be within your legal authority to arrest the woman for assaulting the boy in this instance. Since
he was not attacking her, she was not acting in self-defense. The woman
has, in a sense, acted contemptuously toward the law and the social
contract by assaulting the youth in your presence, and she deserves to
be arrested and charged with a crime. Moreover, the boy deserves to
have his right to be safe from assault exonerated in a court of law.

Yet most participants would feel uneasy arresting the woman, and
few have said they would definitely take this action—unless the woman
insisted on continuing her assaultive behavior despite repeated commands to desist. Partly, we suspect, police officers are embarrassed by
the prospect of presenting respectable-seeming middle-aged women at

the booking desk, for fear of peer criticism that they should be able to "handle" such individuals without resorting to the use of coercive force. Others simply do not think a "mickey mouse" assault such as hers on the boy, which occurred in the heat of a dispute rather than through premeditation, would be taken seriously by a prosecutor or a magistrate, much less a jury. Thus, they see her attack on the boy as unworthy of formal processing through arrest. Generally, many officers refrain from making many arrests that their authority would technically allow them to effect, and the use of some force by disputants is often one of the times when officers would prefer some other disposition to the incident rather than arrest. Research indicates that, in domestic (spousal) disputes particularly, arrest seems an undesirable resolution of the dispute in many officers' minds, even where couples have been fighting physically.[3] This appears to be true regardless of the class or race of the disputants and the officers involved; police are just as reluctant to arrest a lower-class minority male who batters his spouse as they are to arrest a "respectable" upper-class white husband who is battering his. So the fact that most officers would be reluctant to arrest the woman in this scenario probably has to do with more than just the fact that she is a female.

When pushed further about their decision not to arrest her even though she had injured the boy, participants have offered a wide range of justifications for their choice. For example, some have justified not arresting the woman on the grounds of *fair access*, arguing that it would be a poor use of police resources for a police officer to leave the street for an hour or more to process this arrest. If the woman's crime were more serious, if it were the kind that put the entire neighborhood or society in general in fear or if the woman offered serious and sustained resistance to your command to stop assaulting the boy, then her behavior would justify your devoting so much time to this case. However, considering the relatively trivial nature of her actions and the likelihood that she will not repeat her actions once you command her not to do so, it seems right for you to resolve the dispute over the bicycle while remaining available to handle the more serious emergencies that might require your rapid response.

Another line of argument against arrest we have heard is grounded in *public trust*. Defenders of this position claim that arrest—the use of coercive force to compel the woman to come with you to the police station in handcuffs—far exceeds the degree of coercion needed to achieve the most important short-term outcome in the case: that the woman stop clawing and punching at the boy. If you carry yourself with sufficient authority, your voice alone should effectuate this outcome. Certainly, you could intrude yourself between the woman and the boy to end the assault. Arresting the woman when all you want to do is end the assault has, for these officers, the ring of overzealousness (which violates *objectivity* as well).

Finally, they argue that *safety and security* dictates your resolving the case without arrest, since none of the issues regarding the allegations of armed robbery would be addressed by your disappearing from the scene with her under arrest. The main object here is the most serious allegation—armed robbery—and to get caught up in the formalities of arresting her because she raised her hand in anger to the boy is to miss the bigger picture for the scene unfolding in front of you.

On the other side, some participants have defended their decision to arrest the woman, and invoked the standards of *public trust* and *objectivity* to do so. Failing to bring her to judgment before a court would be a way of telling her that the private use of force was permitted as a means for resolving disputes or venting angry feelings, thus violating the boy's trust that you will protect him and vindicate his rights. They also claim that, by not arresting her, the boys might think you lacked objectivity since she was a white adult, and you too are an adult. (This might be a particularly telling point if you, too, are white.)

The fact that experienced police officers can each apply the *fair access, public trust, safety and security*, and *objectivity* standards to the new facts of the scenario and come up with differing conclusions illustrates the degree to which ethical decision-making by police officers is a "means–ends" problem-solving exercise. In our discussions, the standards of ethical police conduct have often been invoked to justify not arresting a lawbreaker on the grounds that the police were created for more important ends than mindless enforcement of law for its own sake. Such logic is central to the *safety and security* standard. When an officer argues that she should reserve her time so that she can respond quickly to the most threatening situations (even if they only occur rarely), the officer reminds us that police presence is a shared social resource made available through public tax monies and distributed on a prioritized basis as needed by all. The officer also alerts us to the fact that police resources are severely limited: one patrol car or walking officer to a beat, and each beat several blocks to several square miles in area.[4] Yet others have argued that the end for which the police were created was the defense of individual rights, not the officer's convenience, and even if it is inopportune or embarrassing to arrest the woman, only in a one-person department could considerations of preserving resources or *safety and security* be invoked to justify not arresting the woman for assault.

OPTION G: *Inform the boy of his right to file a complaint for assault and battery against a woman.*

Although you may not want to arrest the woman for this offense, you may still feel a need to assure the boy that he has access to his legal rights. You can meet this obligation by informing him of his right to seek a criminal complaint against the woman for her assaultive behavior. For some officers, this is often the route they take to resolve disputes, particularly those that involve strong feelings that have led, or might soon lead, to violence. They see the courts as a useful venue for conflicts that are not subject to resolution through their personal, on-the-spot mediation, and that might escalate into a series of attacks and retaliations. Many officers see courts as places where those with valid grievances can get a more thoughtful and deliberative hearing than they can in the few minutes police allocate to each "disturbance call." In that sense, by referring the boy to court, you are providing him with *fair access* to a resource that can give him more satisfaction; you are giving him access to justice. By using the court rather than your own arrest efforts, you are also providing for *safety and security* without overzealously exercising your own authority.

Other officers see referring the youth to a court as an irresponsible "kissing off" of your personal responsibility for controlling the woman's behavior and assuring that her anger will not flare up at another time. Unless the boy chooses to tell his parents about the confrontation and they are willing to accompany him to court (hardly a certainty in many instances), your telling the boy to get the courts to enforce his rights is likely to be useless to him. These participants argue that any protection of his rights in this case is most directly (and therefore best) from you. You must assure yourself and him that the woman has stopped her assault and will not resume it, either after you depart or at some other time or place. Arresting her will surely teach her that violence is not a permissible element in her dispute with him. Anything else is too easily interpreted as tacit approval of her actions.

> **OPTION H:** *Warn the woman that, if she persists in her behavior, you will have to arrest her; separate the two parties; continue your conversations trying to establish the facts regarding her allegations that the bike is stolen and belongs to her son.*

Basically, this option can be thought of as your attempt to educate the woman (and by extension all parties present) about the acceptable limits of behavior, so that you can go back to handling the situation the way you would have before she lost her self-control. The virtues of this approach are that you are not overusing your authority (instead, you are merely issuing a warning about the consequences of her employing illegal behavior), you are protecting the boy from further attempts to harm him and you are still allowing yourself time to find the best solution to the allegations of armed robbery and bike theft. By asserting control over her, you are re-establishing control over the whole situation (which provides safety for all, since you are now very concerned that the boy and his friends will want to retaliate against the woman). You are providing for safety as well as justice. Had the woman seriously injured the boy, you would almost certainly have to place her under arrest, or at least take her name and get a complaint from a court at some later time. However, for many officers, assuring themselves that neither party would resume the fighting would probably suffice. After all, most officers feel they have seen far more serious violence than that described in the scenario. As for the scratches the boy suffered, your compelling the woman to desist and expressing concern for him would probably do much to salve his wound. You might consider asking her to apologize, unless you thought this would inflame feelings again. To repeat an earlier point, if you felt that resolving the allegations of armed robbery was the most important point, you would want to minimize the woman's eruption. If you think the assault is the main thing, then you probably find Option H unsatisfactory.

SUMMARY AND CONCLUSION

By changing the facts of the scenario, we managed to alter the focus of our discussion. In the original example, in which the woman and the boy were tugging at the bicycle and offering their own explanations of its ownership, our discussion centered on issues of credibility, legality and property ownership, as well as the possibility of a serious armed crime having occurred. We explored optional responses that, at bottom, were based on the process of assessing who was more likely to be telling the truth about their relationship to the bike or whether the boy before you seemed likely to have committed a robbery two days previously. The rule of law might delimit what they did in response to your assessments (whether or not you confiscated the bike, arrested the boy or simply returned the bike to him for lack of probable cause to take it into custody), but our considerations primarily revolved around who we believed, who we could trust to leave and return with information, who had witnesses to attest to his or her truthfulness and so on.

In the variation, the woman's assault on the boy focused us more tightly on other issues. We started to think about our obligation to provide protection to victims rather than our obligation to resolve property disputes. Our consideration about whether it was necessary or appropriate to arrest the woman was based less on an assessment of her character than on a prediction about her future actions (that is, about her continuing to be assaultive despite your command to stop attacking the boy). In other words, we were less concerned about who owned the bike or whether we might be dealing with a boy who had robbed from another at knife point, and more concerned about how to control or respond to one party's behavior in the here and now.

Because the potential for a public disturbance as a consequence of this incident is real, Option D, taking the bicycle, inviting a visit to the station and separating the parties, seems to us on balance the best choice, even though it may overstep the strict legal limits of police authority in this case. Others in the criminal justice system (judges, and perhaps prosecutors and juries) will ultimately have to decide where the truth lies in the property dispute, and you would be respecting the standard of *teamwork* by letting this happen. Your responsibility to maintain the participants' safety is at risk of being ignored if you view this incident strictly as a property dispute. Since public order is such a central part of police work, we regard it as important that you take additional action to address that dimension of the incident. Changing the example somewhat helped bring this concern for peacekeeping back into the foreground; it also illuminated the point that there are multiple standards to meet in any policing situation.

NOTES

1. Cited in Charles E. Silberman, *Criminal Violence, Criminal Justice* (New York: Vintage Books, 1980), p. 268.

2. William Ker Muir, Jr., in *Police: Streetcorner Politicians* (Chicago: University of Chicago Press, 1977), pp. 61–64, cites "skid row" as a place where police are more likely to use force as a technique of social control, because so few of its regular residents have much to lose from the threat of arrest or other legal processes.

3. Lawrence W. Sherman and Richard A. Berk, "The Minneapolis Domestic Violence Experiment," *Police Foundation Reports* 1 (April, 1984), pp. 1–8.

4. Such considerations should also remind officers of why it is such a serious dereliction when they "steal" time from the public by leaving their post early, sleeping on duty or finding inventive ways to keep from performing random patrol or responding to radio dispatches.

6

Calling in a Favor

Thus far, we have applied the five standards to evaluate police conduct in two public order situations: a threat to public safety posed by a cocaine-dealing motorcycle gang at a rock concert and a dispute in a park over an allegedly stolen bicycle. Although both of these cases seemed to involve a potentially serious crime (an alleged robbery at knife point; the apparent sale of cocaine), our first obligation in acting as a police officer was to assure that no one got hurt in either incident. In both cases, the social contract dictated that the law be enforced, to the degree that it could, with a principal concern for safety (even that of the suspects). Our concern for safety was not based on our personal knowledge of, relationship with or caring about the individuals involved. Rather, we provided for their safety because it was the duty of a police officer to do so. The basis of our actions, then, should have been strictly professional.

In the scenario that follows, you must select a course of action as a professional that may compete with a personal relationship. The scenario places you as a police officer in a potential conflict between your obligation to uphold the motor vehicle law and your loyalty to a friend who breaks it. We believe that the five standards of police ethics will help resolve some of the conflicts involved, but they may not suffice to reconcile the many competing pulls you may feel. Consider the following scenario:

While at the academy, you were trained that it is against department policy to accept gratuities—discounts, half-priced meals, even a free cup of coffee—on the grounds that, "except for your paycheck, there's no such thing as an honest buck." In practice, however, things are less clear-cut.

For example, it is common among uniformed patrol officers and sergeants to accept free coffee and snacks at a doughnut shop in one of the high-crime areas in your city. Just about all the uniformed officers accept the coffee, sodas, cookies and doughnuts offered freely by the store owner, and the department seems, at bottom, to know but not care that officers are accepting this unpaid-for hospitality.

In the months that you have been assigned to a midnight shift in this neighborhood, you find yourself developing a good personal relationship with the store owner, a man named Teddy. You respect his willingness to work hard, and truly appreciate his generosity in supplying you and your colleagues with a much needed cup of coffee, some food and a warm welcome on your long, sometimes tedious and lonely tours of duty. Correspondingly, he seems genuinely happy to see you as a person as well as to appreciate your willingness to spend your breaks at his establishment. He had been held up at gun point twice in the past, and it makes him feel safer with you there.

Around 3:30 A.M. on a dry, quiet summer night, you pull over a car that has just gone through a red light at approximately 30 mph without stopping or even slowing down. When you approach the vehicle, you recognize the operator as Teddy on his way home from a night's work. He gets out of the vehicle, addresses you by name and reaches out to shake your hand. Teddy tells you he is sorry about the traffic light and says, "Hey, you are not going to give your old buddy here a ticket for a little thing like that, are you?"

Police tend to have a very ambivalent relationship with the general public. Many officers tend to be suspicious of the motives of those who try to befriend them. This appears to be so at least in part because police are streetwise, and trained to believe that guilty people are constantly trying to deceive or keep information from them. Partly, police officers mistrust people because they know that, as powerful authority figures, they attract many individuals who wish to exploit that authority for their personal gain. Also, police are suspicious because they believe that unstable or vicious people are provoked by the badge and uniform into hostile, aggressive acts against them, and thus an officer can never let his or her guard down.

On the other hand, police officers are also known for their good will and generosity. They tend toward talkativeness and love good conversation. Police officers are liked by and trust other public workers, such as nurses, firefighters and emergency medical technicians. They also get along with those who work night shifts, like themselves, such as waitresses, cooks and utility workers. These individuals seem to share a common bond based on the struggle to stay awake at night, being out of sync with the schedule kept by the great majority of people, sudden excitement and a shared experience of seeing human tragedy.

In this scenario, you share a common understanding with the doughnut shop owner. You both work in the early hours before dawn, when most "civilians" are asleep. Like you, he is at risk of attack by criminals, and must deal with the drunks and derelicts who enter his territory. The two of you share your sense of vulnerability and danger, and he appreciates how hard it is to work when others are at home in their warm beds. Now, you must choose how you want to handle his illegal behavior and what you might see as his attempt to exploit your "friendship" to avoid the consequences of his behavior. Here are a few of your options:

OPTION A: Write the citation. Tell him that it is nothing personal; you have to write it as a matter of duty. Continue to accept Teddy's hospitality at his shop if it is offered.

OPTION B: Write the citation. Tell him that it is nothing personal; you have to write it as a matter of duty. Start paying for your coffee and doughnuts at his shop.

OPTION C: Write the citation. Tell him that it is nothing personal; you have to write it as a matter of duty. Stop going to his shop.

OPTION D: Do not write the citation. Tell him he is right about buddies not putting each other in a hard spot, so he needs to drive more carefully in the future. Continue to accept his hospitality as before.

OPTION E: Do not write the citation. Do not respond to his comment about the two of you being buddies. Ask him to drive more carefully in the future. Stop accepting the free coffee and doughnuts or, alternatively, find another place to take your breaks.

OPTION F: Tell him he has put you in an awkward spot by invoking your personal relationship. Tell him to drive more carefully in the future since you will have to cite him if you catch him breaking the law again. Continue to accept coffee and doughnuts at his shop.

OPTION G: Tell him he has put you in an awkward spot by invoking your relationship. Ask him to please drive more carefully in the future since you will have to cite him if you catch him breaking the law again. Begin to alternate the places at which you take your breaks, and pay for your food and coffee at each of the places.

The scenario illustrates the complicated and ambiguous human relationships that police develop as they try to balance their personal lives against their public authority. Law enforcement work is essentially *instrumental*: it is usually a means to achieve some other end. Traffic law, which is at issue here, is enforced primarily to ensure the safe operation of motor vehicles and, secondarily, to promote a general social habit or practice of abiding by law. In short, traffic law enforcement is not done to vindicate lawfulness for its own sake, simply because the law must be obeyed. For many officers, if traffic safety can be attained by other means, this can be seen as acceptable, given the goals of motor vehicle law.

Human relationships, by contrast, have the potential to be *intrinsic* as well as instrumental; in many cases, a relationship with another human being can be an end or good in itself. Human relationships can supply intangible rewards, such as good feelings or a sense of mutual support. Healthy human relationships do not need to be justified for their capacity to achieve any purpose beyond the fact that they satisfy the individuals who have them. They need serve no higher or extrinsic purpose.

Because police officers hold authority and are in theory obligated to exercise it *even against those with whom they have a personal relationship*, they can rarely have a purely intrinsic relationship with anyone other than a close family member. Even with friends to whom they develop a close relationship, the possibility exists that they will find themselves in some circumstances on opposite sides of the law. Officers might find themselves at social events where neighbors or acquaintances are smoking marijuana, or where someone gets behind the wheel of a car after having had too much to drink. Sometimes, they even find themselves having to decide whether to enforce the law or department rules against their own colleagues. (We will address this particular dilemma in the next chapter.) Knowing how to respond in these situations is not easy.

In this scenario, you need to decide how to handle an incident involving someone with whom you have a relatively casual relationship that you have developed at work, not at your home or in your social life. Still, it puts you in the embarrassing position of possibly having to enforce the law against someone who is, by conventional measures, a friend. Let us examine your options in greater detail.

OPTION A: *Write the citation. Tell him that it is nothing personal; you have to write it as a matter of duty. Continue to accept Teddy's hospitality at his shop if it is offered.*

Taking this course of action essentially separates the personal and professional aspects of this incident. Running a red light can be a dangerous action and serious offense, even though (fortunately) nothing happened in this instance. Telling Teddy that there is nothing personal in your citing him makes it clear that you are simply living up to the ethical standards required of a law enforcement officer. By giving him a citation, you respect *fair access* by not giving special favors to friends, fulfill your *public trust* by assuring other drivers and pedestrians that you are keeping them safe from those who operate a vehicle dangerously and live up to the standard of *objectivity* by dealing with the seriousness of Teddy's actions and not your personal attachment to him.

Citing Teddy for running a red light fulfills your duty to enforce the law. Continuing to patronize his stop and accept his coffee without paying indicates that you did not consider his hospitality as a bribe— that is, he was not giving you the coffee as a way to buy immunity from traffic law enforcement. If Teddy continues to offer you coffee and doughnuts gratuitously, this would demonstrate that, in fact, he did not mean them as a bribe. Rather, they came with no strings attached. Conversely, if he did stop offering the coffee for free, you would know that he had meant it as a bribe, and you would have done the right thing by ticketing him to show that you could not be bought for the price of a cup of coffee.[1]

In some ways, Option A could represent an ideal outcome for this scenario. You would have upheld the integrity of the law and shown no favoritism in its execution. Hopefully, Teddy would understand this and not retaliate by cutting off your coffee. Put another way, if all worked well, you would have upheld your *public trust* and not impaired your personal relationship. Yet rarely if ever are ongoing human relationships this structured, and it is hard to imagine such "clean" outcomes emerging from relationships between police officers and the "friends" they make in the course of their work.

To protect officers from compromising situations such as the one depicted in the scenario, most if not all major police departments prohibit the acceptance of gratuities. This policy helps avoid the appearance of favoritism or conflict of interest. Departments also justify prohibiting gratuities on the grounds that they are the "slippery slope" down which officers slide to more serious forms of corruption.[2] Many police administrators believe that officers who develop a tolerance for little gratuities will acquire a taste for bigger gifts (bribes), which are usually offered to police in exchange for overlooking infractions of the law. Trading exemption from law enforcement in exchange for cash, goods, services or favors is a clear violation of *public trust* since the officer involved would be exploiting his or her publicly granted authority for personal, private gain. Few officers need to be convinced that it is wrong to accept cash from a motorist in exchange for overlooking a speeding violation or from a construction company that wants to leave a pile of bricks blocking a thoroughfare, much less from a drug dealer who wants to avoid arrest. If it is true that accepting anything, even a free cup of coffee or a pack of cigarettes, from individuals with an interest in the outcome of police action or inaction can acclimate officers to accepting bribes to protect criminality, then accepting the free cup of coffee and cigarettes should indeed be banned.

However, we find that there is little if any substantial proof that small gratuities are a significant precursor to major police corruption. Although it seems true that almost all officers who eventually accept major bribes began their downward path by accepting small gratuities, apparently the vast majority of officers who resist the temptation to accept major bribes have also accepted gratuities. So it seems that there must be other reasons that some officers take the steps beyond gratuities to corruption, just as only some drinkers become alcoholics.

What we find more troubling about gratuities is that they have a potential to skew the delivery of police services. That is, gratuities can induce officers into unwitting or unintended violations of *fair access*. This standard requires that every citizen receive police services on the basis of need. Since police service is a relatively limited resource, those who receive the benefit of police presence ought to be those who most need it. If police presence is distributed on any basis other than priority of need, it fails to meet the *fair-access* standard.

Let us make this argument more concretely. Imagine that a department in a resource-strapped city can only assign one officer to cover a beat in a high-crime area of the city on the midnight shift. Now, suppose that officer eats dinner at restaurant A each night. Arguably, the patrons and staff of restaurant A are safer, and almost certainly feel safer, from criminal victimization than persons eating or working at restaurants B, C or D, which have no police officer eating there. An atmosphere or sense of safety is a benefit for any business establishment, and can help increase patronage and profits. Some businesses recognize this fact and hire private security officers or a public police officer on privately paid duty, in order to assure the public of a safe shopping, drinking or dining environment.

The hiring of an off-duty officer to serve as a uniformed security guard makes the commercial basis of the relationship between the business establishment and the officer transparent: the business pays a fee for the officer's presence, and the officer is present on active duty to protect the establishment. The exchange is straightforwardly contractual. However, gratuities can be used as a way to obtain the same police presence or attention without overtly contracting for the service. Several national restaurant chains have a policy of offering half-price meals or free coffee to officers who appear *in uniform*. The key, we think, to the in-uniform provision is that only uniformed officers serve as a deterrent to potential criminals or rowdy patrons.

Put another way, these gratuities and discounts are offered with the intention of diverting a public resource (police presence) to a business's benefit (enhanced security). The problem with gratuities in this view is not, as it is with the "slippery slope" argument, that the officer is exploiting his authority for his personal gain (the price of a cup of coffee). Rather, it is that others are exploiting the officer's authority to their personal ends.

Let us offer a final perspective on the issue. Another word for gratuities is tips. They are usually given to waiters and waitresses, hairdressers, taxi drivers, porters and so on—individuals who have performed a personal service for another, possibly with some expectation on the giver's part of being served again by that individual in the future. Most times, however, tips are given impersonally as payment for the immediate service rendered, rather than with an eye to future performance.

In this instance, we see Teddy's free cups of coffee as similar to a conventional "tip." He did not begin offering the coffee and doughnuts to you because of your intrinsic qualities or his affinity for you as a person. Rather, he began offering them to you because you were a uniformed officer driving a marked patrol car, which you parked in his lot. It was the fact of your holding and exercising public authority that qualified you for the free food and coffee. Had you been off duty and out of uniform the first time you entered the shop, neither Teddy, the patrons nor potential robbers would have been able to identify you as a police officer, and thus you would have provided no visible deterrent. Correspondingly, you would have been expected to pay for whatever you ordered.

It would be inaccurate to argue that even now Teddy is offering you coffee and doughnuts as a sign of hospitality, much as he would if you were a guest in his home. Although you might have developed a personal relationship with him over time, his original offer of free coffee and food was part of an implicit bargain: if you entered his premises in uniform and parked your patrol car out front, then you could have coffee and a doughnut "on the house."

However innocent your understanding and his intent, the transaction between the two of you is an exchange of goods and benefits, and thus a form of payment to you which we define as a gratuity, tip or fee for service. As we can imagine, sometimes the expectations implicit in the offer of a gratuity are not as innocent as those depicted in the scenario we have been analyzing. For example, some business establishments offer police officers free or discount service with the expectation that the officers will not ticket illegally parked cars of customers shopping in the store. Others will expect officers who accept gratuitous goods or services to overlook minor violations, such as placing sales tables on the sidewalk without a permit, leaving trash barrels uncovered or receiving deliveries during hours when trucks are prohibited.

Please review Option A again. Its final portion says that you would "continue to accept the owner's hospitality at his shop if it is still offered." If you felt comfortable in accepting his gratuitous coffee and doughnuts after you had cited him for running a red light, then your rejection of the parallel between the free coffee and the "tip" is clear: despite having cited him for a traffic violation that was within your discretion to overlook (that is, having "served him badly"), you could still comfortably accept his free coffee and doughnuts. Clearly you have separated out your citing him from your patronizing his shop.

All this having been said, and despite our objection to gratuities because of their potential to generate favoritism, we know few officers who would actually cite a friend such as Teddy for a traffic violation under these circumstances. Experienced officers say that they might have to cite him if he caused an accident or if he were abusive, but to follow our referee analogy, a majority of those officers we have worked with invoke the "no harm, no foul" principle sometimes applied by referees in hockey, basketball or football. Since they might well give a break to a stranger in these circumstances, they think it needlessly formal to cite a friend for a relatively "harmless" violation.

> **OPTION B:** *Write the citation. Tell him that it is nothing personal; you have to write it as a matter of duty. Start paying for your coffee and doughnuts at his shop.*

Paying for your own coffee and doughnuts after the incident would be a way to establish with Teddy that you felt his comments were intended to exploit your personal relationship for favors. His saying, "You're not going to give your old buddy here a ticket" could be interpreted to imply that the free coffee was not only meant to attract you to his premises, but to buy your good will in the event he ran afoul of the law. Continuing to patronize his store but insisting on paying for your coffee reaffirms your independence, as well as your lack of remorse at having performed your duty.

Although it is virtuous, Option B, like Option A, is also somewhat formal and extreme. In a sense, insisting on paying for your own coffee after the incident is tantamount to telling Teddy that, because of his tasteless comment, you no longer feel you can be his friend, even if up to that time your friendship had been based primarily on a non-corrupt reciprocity of sincere interests and mutual desires rather than his devious attempts to manipulate you. Surely, if he makes the first move and begins to charge you for coffee, then you must pay for it or take your business elsewhere (see Option C). As we mentioned in our discussion of Option A, if he does withdraw the offer of free coffee, then he might have meant it as a way to buy immunity from law enforcement. However, it may be that he is charging you for coffee as a way of saying that he respects your professionalism and wants to keep you from getting into the same predicament again. Until you know with certainty why he is charging you, it is unclear whether you should feel insulted or complimented.

In the end, this question of whether Teddy should continue to offer, and you should continue to accept, free coffee reveals the potential for human misunderstanding when social relationships overlap with profes-

sional authority relationships. Once again, on balance, it seems better
not to have begun taking the coffee.

OPTION C: *Write the citation. Tell him that it is nothing personal; you
have to write it as a matter of duty. Stop going to his shop.*

Let us assume that Teddy understands that your citing him is indeed
"nothing personal," and that he continues to offer you free coffee and
doughnuts as before. You might still feel reluctant to accept his offer-
ings. Your grounds for this reluctance might be the fact that you feel
he tried to misuse your "friendship" to keep you from writing a citation.
Having performed your duty in the face of this undue influence, you
may now feel obliged to put yourself on an impersonal basis with the
man so he cannot repeat his behavior. One way to guarantee that distance
is not to patronize his establishment. You may also simply feel insulted
by his actions and not want to be with him again. Any of these reasons
would be based on an understandable human impulse. We know of at
least one officer who, in fact, did exactly this in a similar situation.

Ironically, however, boycotting Teddy's shop to avoid contact, no
matter how principled your intentions, might violate *fair access* and
objectivity. After all, if your uniformed presence or its anticipation is
a benefit to every business because it can serve as a deterrent to crime
and a confidence builder for staff and patrons, you cannot justify depriving Teddy of at least random official visits to his shop. The emphasis
here is on the term "official." As we have explained, police are a public
resource to which all must have, or should have, *fair access*, that is,
access on the basis of need. Personal feelings are not a valid grounds
on which to withhold *fair access*. To allow your subjective reactions
to Teddy's words to deprive him of at least a share of your random
patrol or break time would violate the requirement of *objectivity*, that
is, the need to overcome personal feelings that distort the delivery of
police services to those who need them.

Some officers we have known argue that the shop owner still has
access to police services via the telephone, or through the other officers
who continue to take advantage of his distributing gratuities. Emergency
police telephone numbers do in fact go a long way toward providing
fair access to a wide number of citizens. Beyond that, these participants
have argued, officers are free to spend their break times where they
wish, and if an officer prefers the food at one restaurant over another,

appreciates a discount or simply dislikes eating at a particular establishment, neither the department nor ethics trainers should interfere in the officer's freedom of association.

This is an argument that is difficult to refute, and in practice we would not compel an officer to eat in an establishment if he or she had a poor relationship with the proprietor. However, let us go at this issue from a somewhat different, more formal perspective, if only for what it can teach us about the levels of meaning attached to the concept of *fair access*. Consider that most basic of police functions, random patrol. For most of us, when we picture the police, it is an image of uniformed officers driving around in patrol cars, responding to calls, doing traffic law enforcement, sometimes getting out of their vehicles and walking, checking doors and windows, talking to neighborhood residents and so forth. Despite the many innovations in policing, random patrol is still one of the most frequently performed activities among uniformed police officers.

Unlike "directed patrol," which is targeted at particular locations (for example, nabbing drivers who chronically fail to stop at a particular intersection) or focused on a particular problem (for example, spotting pickpockets at a shopping mall), random patrol is meant to be just that, *random*. It should, at some point, reach virtually all the citizens and locations on a beat. Random patrol theory is based on the assumption that the randomness is a deterrent to criminals because they never know when the police will appear. If you avoid Teddy's shop because of a personal peeve, you would deprive him and his customers of a benefit to which they, like all other citizens, are entitled to receive.[3]

Conversely, your constant patronage of Teddy's shop prior to the incident was also a violation of *fair access* in respect to the other eating establishments on your beat (unless, of course, his shop was the *only* place to get coffee on your beat during the midnight shift). An ideal application of *fair access* would have you randomly take your breaks or eat your on-duty meals at each of the eateries, not just the one or ones that offered you a discount or a freebie. After all, every restaurant or coffee shop pays its taxes and is entitled to *fair access* to police officers, that is, access on the basis of need rather than the officer's preference for whom he or she will serve.

Just as you should not have made Teddy a favorite before he ran the red light, you should not penalize him because you feel he has strained your friendship. Just as you may feel a formal obligation to cite him because of your duty to uphold the law, you should feel a formal obligation to patrol around his shop, enter it, stay in it occasionally and offer all the services and benefits you offer to the other shopkeepers and restaurant owners on your beat—no more, but no less. As we have said earlier, *objectivity* may be the hardest standard to live up to.

> **OPTION D:** *Do not write the citation. Tell him he is right about buddies not putting each other in a hard spot, so he needs to drive more carefully in the future. Continue to accept his hospitality as before.*

Reminding Teddy of the importance of driving carefully, rather than giving him a citation, has the advantage of allowing you to maintain your professional stance as a law enforcement officer without treating him as if you had no friendship. It strikes a balance between your law enforcement role and your personal relationship. Option D recognizes that police have broad discretion in the exercise of their work. The traffic laws allow an officer a choice between written citations and verbal warnings to violators, and some states even permit the intermediate step of a written warning. Many laws are written in language that allows, but does not compel, officers to arrest or cite if they detect a violation. Therefore, choosing to give Teddy only a verbal warning is almost certainly within your authority. So long as a verbal warning is something you are likely to do for other violators in similar circumstances, and not simply something you are doing especially for Teddy because he is a friend, you have met the standard of *fair access*. In other words, if you would give the same "break" to any deserving person and not just your favorites, then you have your discretion fairly and objectively.

As with the earlier options, by choosing Option D, you have also met the requirements of *public trust*, since you have told Teddy that, despite his friendship with police officers or the fact that he has shown them hospitality, he cannot and should not violate traffic laws. Neatly, you have upheld the safety goals of the traffic law, yet not imperiled your friendship by issuing a citation to uphold them. So long as you consider enforcement of the traffic laws as a means to insure public safety and not as an end in itself, warning Teddy might accomplish as much as writing the citation.

Our experience has been that a majority of experienced officers select Option D as their preferred response to the situation. To determine whether they were choosing D because of the fact that Teddy's actions did not harm, or by contrast they chose it because of their personal relationship to Teddy, we asked participants whether they would continue to choose Option D if a second car had been coming through the intersection and was forced to swerve sharply to avoid Teddy's vehicle. In other words, would they still seek to preserve Teddy's friendship in those new circumstances, or would his behavior become the controlling factor in their decision?

Interestingly, a majority of officers have said that they would not cite him even in these new circumstances, although they say they would have to cite him if his driving resulted in a collision. In defense of not citing Teddy despite the near-miss with the second vehicle, the participants have argued that no one was hurt in the incident, even if everyone was a bit scared for a moment. Probably, the second car would drive on, and the incident would be forgotten. We have then asked these participants whether their actions would be affected if the second car stopped and its driver asked what the officers were going to do about Teddy's having run the red light. Would those officers be able merely to give Teddy a verbal warning if the other driver were standing within earshot, or would they feel compelled to write a citation because an aggrieved citizen was watching? Although most participants are slow to answer this question, and no clear consensus has emerged on how to handle this variation, we raise it to test whether the participants' sense of their permissible discretion is somehow reduced when witnesses or complainants are present. As well, we think that any inherent favoritism that might be involved in letting Teddy go with a warning is revealed by introducing a complaining witness into the situation. If a participant is suddenly uncomfortable in letting Teddy go with a third party present, then he or she may have been using permissible discretion only as a way to play favorites. Again, changing the hypothetical circumstances helps us evaluate whether we are primarily considering the act, the consequences of the act for others or our relationship to the actor.

To conclude our examination of Option D, let us consider its final sentence: "Continue to accept his hospitality as before." We ask participants how they think Teddy would interpret their accepting coffee and doughnuts after issuing a verbal warning, but not writing a citation. Do they assume that he would think his hospitality had earned him the warning rather than the citation, or would he understand that they felt there was no connection between the coffee and the "break" they had given him, because they would give the same latitude to other offenders as well? Certainly, continuing to take the coffee if one knows that it has not purchased any favoritism is acceptable. If it has purchased exemption from law enforcement, it was wrong to take it before the incident, and it would be wrong to take it afterward.

To determine whether the use of discretion to Teddy's advantage was based on the lack of harm in his actions, the likelihood of giving the same "break" to a stranger or the personal connection between participants and Teddy, we ask them to imagine whether they would let him go with a verbal warning if, when they stopped him, Teddy sounded hostile and said something like, "Friends don't screw friends." Would they still tell him he was correct, ask him to drive carefully and maintain their previous relationship, including the taking of the doughnuts and coffee?

Many participants react to this new variation by saying that the man's changed attitude would cost him any "break" they were willing to give him. Others, a minority, remain consistent and remind their fellow participants that any citizen, like any cop, could have a bad day. If you sincerely like the man, you would not let his temper in one weak moment destroy your relationship, although it might teach you something about the limits of his character. *Objectivity* would require that an officer not let his friendship lead him to *punish* someone because that person had tried to take advantage of a friendship any more than he or she should excuse a person from punishment just because that person was a friend. Objectivity requires that Teddy's offense and not his demeanor determine the officer's behavior in this instance. Legally, there is no such charge as "contempt of cop," even if more than one participant has confessed to us having arrested persons or issued citations to them because they flunked the "attitude test"—that is, they failed to show expected respect for the officer.

Citing a motorist because of her attitude rather than the nature of the offense would also be a violation of *public trust*. Officers would be using their official authority to achieve a personal benefit, in this instance, the vindication of their own egos. If the offender deserved a penalty because the violation was serious, she should receive one. If she received one to teach her to speak meekly to police officers, this would be a violation of *public trust*.

Some officers understand the philosophical point here but reject it as unrealistic. They argue that you might continue to give a break to an abusive friend or fellow officer but that it is unwise to give a break to an abusive citizen you do not know, even if failing to do so violates the formal requirement of *public trust*. The basis for this argument is that breaks are reserved primarily for those who show remorse or some other indication that they have learned from their confrontation with "the law" not to break it in the future. Those persons who demonstrate hostility or contempt in the presence of an officer are, in a sense, anarchists; they fail to acknowledge that they have violated the terms of the social contract. Defying the agent of the contract (the police) is tantamount to defying civilization itself. This is an indicator of the "ungovernability" of the individual (making him a threat to the officer) and his incivility (making him a threat to others). His irrationality in "mouthing off" to a police officer may even indicate that he is a threat to himself (either because he is drunk, under the influence of drugs or mentally unstable). Whatever his problem, he needs and deserves police intervention and the exercise of authority to restore his governability and reason.[4]

We acknowledge the power of this argument. However, too often we have discussed with officers their feeling that anyone (even another officer, say, one they have stopped driving drunk off-duty) who mouths off at them "is gone" (presumably into custody). This is simply a matter of saving face or self-image, rather than a thought-out position having to do with the offender's irrationality, governability or threat to self or others. The damage is to the officer's ego or feelings. *Objectivity* precludes an officer's introduction of personal feelings as a grounds for official action.

> **OPTION E:** *Do not write the citation. Do not respond to his comment about the two of you being buddies. Ask him to drive more carefully in the future. Stop accepting the free coffee and doughnuts or, alternatively, find another place to take your breaks.*

As with Option D, not writing a citation is within your discretion, and it respects the fact that you had a relationship with the man. No longer accepting gratuitous coffee and doughnuts is intended to serve as a clear signal that you felt he was trying to take advantage of your relationship when he reminded you that friends do not cite friends. In many ways, this is a very acceptable option: it avoids ingratitude for his past favors, teaches him not to compromise your professionalism and frees you from the obligations of friendship or favors if he repeats his offense in the future. However, this option leaves the definition of your relationship to your now ex-friend potentially unclear. We think it necessary to address directly his offer of a handshake and remarks about "buddies" if you feel they have compromised your relationship. We think the next option meets that requirement more directly.

OPTION F: *Tell him he has put you in an awkward spot by invoking your personal relationship. Tell him to drive more carefully in the future since you will have to cite him if you catch him breaking the law again. Continue to accept coffee and doughnuts at his shop.*

This option appears to meet both the standards of friendship and police ethics (assuming he keeps offering the free coffee and food). You have reminded a citizen of the importance of observing the law and thus met the standard of *public trust*. By addressing directly the fact that he appeared to be playing on your relationship and telling him he was wrong to do so, you have maintained your integrity and upheld *fair access* (no favorites, no favors). By continuing to accept his hospitality should he offer it, you continue to assert that you are not corrupted by his offer, since you have told him that the next time you would have to cite him. Also, you have maintained your friendship intact.

Despite its virtues, we seek two drawbacks to this option. First, it implies that you will continue to spend most of your break time at your friend's restaurant, which is not fair to the other restaurants on your beat (should any be open). Secondly, your friend might indeed violate the law a second time, and you will then have to face having to cite someone who has been gracious to you in the past; you are merely buying time before you have to face the discomfort you avoided this time. It thus seems to us that an even more preferable course is to choose the next option.

OPTION G: *Tell him he has put you in an awkward spot by invoking your relationship. Tell him to drive more carefully in the future since you will have to cite him if you catch him breaking the law again. Begin to alternate the places at which you take your breaks, and pay for your food and coffee at each of the places.*

By this point, you can probably deduce for yourself why we think this is the best of the offered options. It meets the goal of upholding public safety through traffic law enforcement, thus upholding *public trust*, while respecting *safety and security*. By not playing favorites or punishing "betrayals" by friends, you are observing both *fair access* and *objectivity*. Choosing this option sustains your professional integrity and demeanor, and leaves the door open to continue your friendship on the basis of respect.

Having come this far with our argument, we hope that you see that it would be better never to have taken Teddy's free coffee and doughnuts in the first place. That way, your independence and integrity could never be called to question. We acknowledge, however, that you might have found yourself in the same awkward spot had you developed a personal friendship with Teddy even if you had been paying for everything you ordered. Had you consistently refused his free offers but, over the months, developed a familiarity, respect and trust in each other, he might still have reminded you that friends do not give friends citations. Having paid for your coffee is no guarantee of insulation against the demands and complications of friendship. Say that, instead of it being Teddy, the individual whose car you stopped turned out to be an old school chum or even a cousin. Surely, gratuities would not be a factor here, but you would still probably feel it nearly impossible to cite the offender.

The essential conflict in this scenario has been between your public duties and your personal relationships. That the personal relationship with Teddy is cemented by an exchange of goods and benefits only adds to the dilemma. In the next chapter, we examine a scenario in which the essential conflict between the performance of duty and the pull of personal relationships is connected to much higher stakes than a free cup of coffee or the issuance of a summons for a simple traffic offense.

NOTES

1. As we have noted elsewhere, what makes a gratuity a bribe is the spirit in which it is offered and the understanding with which it is accepted. If a gratuity is offered by a merchant to buy exemptions from law enforcement or is accepted by the officer with an understanding that some favor is required in return, then the gratuity functions as a bribe. Michael Feldberg, "Gratuities, Corruption and the Democratic Ethos of Policing: The Case of the Free Cup

of Coffee," *Moral Issues in Police Work*, Frederick A. Elliston and Michael Feldberg, eds. (Totowa, N.J.: Rowman and Allenheld, 1985), p. 267.

2. Lawrence W. Sherman, "Becoming Bent: Moral Careers of Corrupt Policemen," ibid, pp. 251–65.

3. Currently, there is significant doubt about the effectiveness of random patrol as a deterrent to crime. See, for example, George Kelling, Tony Pate, Duane Dieckman and Charles E. Brown. *The Kansas City Preventive Patrol Experiment: A Summary Report* (Washington, D.C.: Police Foundation, 1974).

4. Muir observed of Laconia's police officers that they, too, took the "attitude test" very seriously. Although from the social contract perspective, the test may be an impermissible loss of objectivity or violation of the public trust by the officer, Muir argues that many officers view a citizen's attitude as a test of the likelihood that the citizen will abide by the law and submit to commands by the officer. As such, the verbal behaviors and attitudes expressed by the citizen may well be a clue to whether the individual poses a threat to the officer or others. A show of authority such as arrest or citation may bring a potentially ungovernable and thus dangerous person to his senses, or pre-emptively bring him under control—thus maintaining the public trust. William Ker Muir, Jr., *Police: Streetcorner Politicians* (Chicago: University of Chicago Press, 1977), pp. 156–57.

7

Child Molester

One feature of police work that makes it morally interesting and an ethical challenge to those who perform it is that much of an officer's activity is done out of public view. Working alone, or only with a partner, police officers usually perform their duties with little if any direct supervision.[1] Most officers only account for their actions *post facto*, in the form of a written report or court testimony, usually to persons who have not actually witnessed the event. Although such freedom from direct oversight presents opportunities to use discretion creatively, it also offers temptations to exceed authority or even to abuse it. Individual officers are often free to present a distorted version of events to justify a needless or illegal arrest, to assure the conviction of a lawbreaker despite the weakness of the evidence against him or her or to protect oneself or a partner from allegations of misbehavior.[2] Since much of police work is done behind the closed doors of homes or apartments, in squad cars, in the holding cells or interrogation rooms of police stations, on darkened streets and alleys or behind trees and buildings, officers can easily reframe and describe events and their own behaviors to fit their needs and purposes.

For many reasons, the formal or written accounts police give of their behavior are not frequently challenged by members of the public. Some of those stopped, questioned, searched or arrested are ignorant of their rights to file a complaint about police behavior, or have no desire to irritate the officer further. Others, even though they know their rights, lack faith that police administrators or courts will credit their complaints, or that public officials would willingly discipline each other. To maintain public confidence, virtually all major police departments have created internal affairs units, which investigate allegations of officer wrong-doing, abuse and discourtesy toward the public as well as disciplinary complaints against officers filed by superiors. Apparently, however, the great majority of the public's complaints about police officer behavior continue never to be brought to these internal affairs units. During criminal trials, the courts can serve to review police behavior during a search, arrest or interrogation, but since only a small minority of arrests ever result in a complete trial (that is, most are settled through a dropping of charges or a plea of guilty), the courts in effect review only a tiny fraction of police/citizen contacts. Thus, the moral burden of both be-having well in the field and telling the truth about that behavior in reports or testimony falls to officers themselves. In police work, of course, the pressures to alter facts to fit circumstances can be great.

In the next example, you are asked to consider whether there are circumstances under which, as a police officer, you might justifiably cover up or lie under oath in a courtroom, or in testimony before an internal affairs hearing, about the misconduct of a fellow officer.

Your partner and you are detectives working in plainclothes. For several days, you have been staking out an elementary school playground where an adult male reportedly has been approaching the children. One particular morning, you have watched a man in his car parked alongside the school yard. When he calls a little girl over to his car and she approaches him on the driver's side, you exit from your unmarked vehicle and approach his vehicle from the pas-senger side so he cannot see you easily in his rear view mirror. When you get just behind his car on the passenger side, you observe that he has his pants open, and he is holding his erect penis in his right hand while talking to the little girl. With his left hand, he is stroking the girl's hair.

You call for your partner over the radio and move to arrest the suspect. Showing him your badge, you order him to close his pants and get out of his car. You handcuff him and place him in the back of your unmarked vehicle, while your partner returns the girl to the safekeeping of school administrators. After telling the suspect of his right to remain silent, you begin interrogating him, recording his name and address and so forth, while awaiting your partner's return.

When your partner comes back, he gets in the rear of your vehicle with the suspect (a violation of department regulations, unless there is reason to believe that the passenger is suicidal). You remind your partner that riding in the back is a violation of the rules, but he stays there anyway, tells you to drive to the station and, turning to the suspect, calls him a "maggot." As you drive, your partner starts punching the suspect repeatedly in the face and the crotch. He even leans back and, bracing himself against the car door, kicks the suspect in the chest and shoulders with the heel of his shoe. When the suspect turns to avoid the blows, your partner kicks him in the back and kidney areas. Throughout this beating, the suspect offers no resistance of any kind. You hear the sounds of the beating and, looking in the rear view mirror, you see your partner striking the suspect. After about a minute, you pull the vehicle over, open the rear door and persuade your partner to get out of the back seat and come sit beside you in the front.

After the suspect is booked and in a holding cell, your partner tells you he will write a report that includes the assertion that the child molester forcefully resisted arrest and sustained injuries during the scuffle to handcuff him. He tells you that he will write the report and sign it, and that you do not have to be associated with its contents.

At his trial, the offender pleads guilty to child molestation charges and is sentenced to three years in prison, to be served at a treatment center for sexual offenders. Soon afterwards, your partner is sued by the offender for physical abuse and injury. Claiming kidney damage, loss of two teeth, civil rights violations and psychological trauma, the convicted molester is asking a civil (not a criminal) court for an award of $2 million from your department and $500,000 from your partner. You receive a subpoena from the court to appear at the trial. In addition, the Internal Affairs Division will launch its own investigation of the allegations, and they inform you that you will be called in to make a statement under oath at a hearing about the events. If the department finds sufficient grounds to believe that your partner acted brutally, he will be suspended or, more likely, fired; if the civil jury finds that he was abusive, he may be forced to sell his home and car to pay the award to the victim. You may also be disciplined for failure to protect your prisoner. Comments in the locker room by other officers make it clear that, given the nature of the victim, they expect you to do whatever is necessary to protect your partner from being held accountable, as well as to "cover your own ass."

Many officers report finding this scenario difficult to deal with because it offers no clearly good choices, only ones that are more or less discomforting. Among the options that have been suggested for dealing with your dilemma are:

OPTION A: Testify falsely in court and at your department's internal affairs hearing that the suspect violently resisted arrest and sustained his injuries when your partner subdued him. Deny that the injuries occurred when your partner was in the back of the patrol car.

OPTION B: Tell the truth in any event, regardless of peer pressure, your partner's wishes or your own material interest in covering up the truth.

OPTION C: Ask your partner's permission to tell the truth. If he grants it, testify honestly and accurately. However, if he asks you to stick by the story in his report that the offender resisted arrest, go along with his wishes.

OPTION D: Tell the court and investigators a mixture of truth and lies: stick to the false story that the offender resisted arrest, but acknowledge that your partner violated regulations by traveling in the back seat with him. Justify this decision by asserting that the offender seemed depressed, that you were worried that he might inflict harm on himself and your partner's riding in the back seemed the best preventive to self-mutilative behaviors. Claim that you do not know what happened in the back seat because you were driving the car and paying attention to the road and your police radio, and that you assume that the offender's injuries must have been sustained when he struggled to resist arrest.

As with the previous scenarios, most of the ethical standards come into some degree of play in this case. *Fair access* is relevant here, since one could make a case that, if you lie to protect your partner, the child molester will be denied access to a fair hearing to decide whether he deserves compensation for his injuries. Regardless of how an officer feels personally about an offender (the *objectivity* standard applies even to child molesters) and however much emotion might dictate otherwise, each offender, as a member of society, is entitled to police efforts to protect his or her life, property and rights—even as the offender is being subdued, and despite his or her efforts to resist authority. Of course, you tried to protect the offender from the beating when it occurred, since you intervened and convinced your partner to stop the beating. However, now, by lying under oath to protect your partner from departmental discipline or civil liability for his wrongdoing, you have deprived the child molester of access to a fair hearing on the merits of his case against your partner. You would also have contributed to a departmental climate that might erode protection of suspected (but presumedly innocent) child molesters in the future.

One could argue as well that, on a broader level, not telling the truth would violate *public trust*. Part of the police obligation to protect the public from crime and violence is met by protecting the public from abuse by the police themselves. If officers conspire to protect each other from accounting for their possible misconduct, they leave the public vulnerable to repeat incidents of misconduct by those officers whose bad behavior they conceal.[3] In respecting the demands of loyalty to protect fellow officers, individual police officers can violate their oath to protect the public, particularly its more despised elements.

The *public trust* standard is centrally involved in another sense as well. As we have noted so many times previously, members of the public, and especially those in secure custody, are comparatively powerless against police officers, that is, are at the officers' mercy. Even vicious criminals, once in custody, are vulnerable to (and thus entitled to protection against) police misuse of power and authority. The constitutional doctrine of separation of powers formally assigns the meting out of punishments to the judiciary, and execution of that punishment is statutorily assigned in every state to the correctional system, which is usually a part of the executive. Legally, then, the police can neither determine nor execute a sentence. The curbstone justice that your partner inflicted on the child molester reminds us that, in certain circumstances, the police can violate *public trust* by causing harm or pain to known offenders. Most law-abiding citizens worry only that police will mistakenly harm individuals who have broken no law, but who may have caused police officers annoyance or discomfort in some way, or even merely said the wrong thing at the wrong time. However, it is well to remember that, under the separation of powers doctrine, *everyone*, even the factually guilty, is supposed to be punished only after a full, fair and public trial.

The third standard, which enjoins police officers to balance law enforcement with a concern for safety and security, seems not to be implicated in this scenario. However, *teamwork*, the fourth standard, is seen by many persons to be at the core of this scenario. In one respect, teamwork is an issue here because of your partner's taking it upon himself to punish the suspect. In the metaphor of sports from which the teamwork analogy is drawn, your partner is "hogging the ball" from his other teammates in the criminal justice system. Under the *teamwork* standard, prosecutors and judges are part of the same criminal justice team as police officers, and are dependent on the police for accurate reports of truthful information about a case so that they can make their most enlightened and effective decisions about how to perform their functions, that is, how to do justice in each case. As such, the requirements of teamwork—cooperation, communication and co-ordination—compel the officer to reveal the truth to department investigators and the civil court.

In this scenario, the formal demands of criminal justice system team-work compete with a more commonplace notion of police teamwork that requires unquestioned loyalty to one's partner. Ironically, the child molester is trying to use the courts and the internal affairs unit of your department, players usually defined as your teammates, to obtain a judgment of wrongdoing against your partner (who *clearly* is your team-mate). Additionally, you might even be in some trouble with your department if your partner is held accountable. You could be disciplined for not reporting fully and accurately what happened in the back of your patrol car, or for allowing it to happen in the first place. You are thus faced not only with a conflict between telling the truth under oath and maintaining loyalty to your partner, but between telling the truth under oath and protecting your self-interest. This scenario forces you to define who is truly "on your team," and to which teammates you owe the obligations of teamwork: with whom, if anyone, you should coordinate, cooperate and communicate about what happened after the arrest of the child molester.

Finally, the standard of *objectivity* clearly applies here. Exercising *public* authority, police officers must set aside personal feelings, such as revulsion, toward particular individuals, must hold in check the desire for revenge or retribution on behalf of innocent victims and must refrain from prejudging what a suspected offender deserves or is likely to receive as punishment. In this case, most police officers with whom we have discussed this scenario feel that the molester's rough handling by your partner was a violation of his rights and the ethical standards of police work, yet the minimum punishment he deserved. Some thought it was the *only* serious punishment he would receive. Many officers are themselves parents and found it hard to blame your partner for doing something they might do (or do even more of) if the victim was their own child. In sum, *objectivity* is particularly tested in this scenario.

The injunction to *objectivity*, however, precisely requires police of-ficers to ignore as best they can their subjective identification with victims, their personal political beliefs, their individual moral values and other elements that might excite their emotions to the point of overusing their authority or failing in some other way to perform their duty in a legal manner. The problem you face in this case is whether your partner's loss of objectivity and control deserves punishment or disciplining, and whether you should risk the appearance of disloyalty to him (with all of its attendant risks) if your testimony in court or to investigators is used against him.

You have a personal stake in whether you take your partner's side or that of his accuser. Telling a lie to protect your partner seems in your immediate self-interest, since if he is cleared of the molester's charges, you are safe from departmental discipline and your colleagues' potential accusations of betrayal. There are reasons having to do with your own survival that may encourage you to lie on behalf of your partner. Covering up for him allows you to continue to function effectively among your fellow officers. Were you to fail to show solidarity and were you to side with a "maggot" against a partner, you would certainly face ostracism by a large segment of your fellow detectives and uniformed patrol officers. The "code of secrecy" described by Westley[4] still applies to some degree in most departments, especially in incidents such as the one described in this scenario. Had you discovered your partner dealing heroin or breaking into and stealing from retail premises in uniform, you would be freed from the obligations to cover for your partner's misdeeds, but officers are supposed to cover for each other when a department, a prosecutor or a civilian charges a fellow officer with "harmless" violations, such as sleeping on duty, receipt of small gratuities, misrepresentation of events in written reports, use of limited but excessive force against known wrongdoers or courtroom perjury to obtain a conviction, in other words, actions that are forbidden, but performed in pursuit of "good" ends, or ends that involve mere personal convenience and not gross violations of law.

This obligation to cover "harmless" rules violations by fellow officers is strongest with a partner or squad member, with friends on the department and colleagues of equal rank, but applies to some degree to every member of one's own department and even to officers from other departments. Some officers report a sense of certainty that, by "giving away" a partner or colleague in a situation such as the one described in the scenario, a police officer would become a pariah within his or her department and could no longer depend on fellow officers for backup assistance in the field. Without this connection to other officers, the officer in question would be vulnerable and thus less effective, for he or she would no longer take life-threatening risks on behalf of vulnerable members of the public. For example, one might not try to rescue a rape victim from a gang of thugs if it required taking on the gang, since there would be a strong possibility that fellow officers would not arrive quickly enough, if at all, to help you subdue the violators. When it comes to maintaining the code of loyalty, some officers believe, it is not simply that one "goes along to get along"; one goes along to survive. However, *objectivity, fair access* and *public trust* require that your decisions be based on the full range of your professional obligations to serve others and not just on the narrow concerns of self-interest. In this scenario, you must determine whether the risks of truthfulness are justified by the ethical imperatives of your office.

Put differently, this scenario directly raises the question of whether there are ever morally justifiable excuses for police lying. Is it permissible for police (or anyone else) to lie to achieve a good end, such as saving a partner's career for a forgivable mistake or to assure the conviction of a known wrongdoer? Is it more seriously wrong to lie under oath than in routine social interaction? Are police under a higher obligation to tell the truth than other members of society or other agents of government? Is telling the truth about duty-related matters a logical extension of the five standards of ethical police work? Carl Klockars has argued that police can lie to achieve the legitimate ends of police work, such as making false promises that you will let a hostage taker leave without arrest if only he will free his victims unharmed.[5] However, does lying to protect a colleague fall under the definition of permissible lies? Having indicated which standards are involved in evaluating your courses of action, and having touched on the special issue of lying, let us look in turn at each of the options enumerated above.

OPTION A: *Testify falsely in court and at your department's internal affairs hearing that the suspect violently resisted arrest and sustained his injuries when your partner subdued him. Deny that the injuries occurred when your partner was in the back of the patrol car.*

In many respects, this is the easiest course to follow, even though it involves lying. As long as your partner agrees to stick to a similar story, there is, in reality, little chance that the child molester will win his suit against your partner. After all, it is his word against yours and your partner's, that is, the word of a convicted felon with an apparent psy-

chiatric disorder against that of two police officers. Both the jury and
the judge are more likely to be sympathetic to your partner than to his
accuser. The department's own internal affairs investigators are unlikely
to pursue the factual truth of this case to its last shred of evidence, both
because your partner would already have been exonerated in a court of
law, and because they are likely sympathetic to your partner's actions
even if they suspect that he was guilty of violating the offender's rights
and department regulations.

You would not be alone if you felt that your partner overreacted but
that many human beings (even you) might have done the same on a given
day. One way to evaluate whether you are required to "blow the whistle" on your partner's treatment of the molester is to ask whether your
partner had a persistent record of abusing prisoners, or was this the first
and only incident of its kind. If he was someone who has, in the past, lost
control with prisoners, you might want to find a way to assure that he is
retrained, counseled, disciplined or even removed from the police force,
but if this instance of overreaction is an isolated case, many officers have
argued, you might find grounds to give him the benefit of the doubt. To
some participants, it has seemed unfair that your partner's livelihood, his
personal property and his standing in the community and the department
should be lost because of one mistake. Surely, they argue, if the practice
of holding police officers to very high standards can lead to consequences more extreme than those imposed on civilians who commit the
same acts, this is such a case. By lying, in other words, you might be
able to protect your partner from the injustice of extreme punishment for a
wrongful, but understandable act.

Others argue that, from the perspective of the social contract and the
standards of police ethics derived from it, your partner's action was
intolerable, and you should not protect him from the consequences of
his actions. Excessive use of force by police officers undermines the
very purpose for which the social contract was created: protection of
citizens from injury or loss imposed by those who are more powerful
or more ruthless than themselves. As agents of government, police
officers are empowered to use force *in defense and only in defense* of
the rights, safety and security of citizens. As public agents, they must
use their authority to protect and preserve private rights. If the actions
of government agents make citizens more vulnerable to loss or harm
than they would be if no government agent were present, then those

agents' actions are contrary to the purposes for which government authority was created. Such is the argument contained in the Declaration of Independence, and such is the logic of social contract theory.

Similarly, those who say you must tell the truth in this instance point out that, if it was wrong for your partner to injure a member of the public unnecessarily, it is wrong for you to stand by and allow him to inflict those injuries, even if they are inflicted on a child molester. As guardians of citizens, police officers are obligated to undertake risks to protect vulnerable citizens, without reference to the deserts or social "worth" of the citizen. One might even argue that the less valued the citizen, the more important that police be the ones to take responsibility for intervening on his or her behalf. After all, the more competent, successful and attractive a citizen, the more likely he or she is to have personal resources and the ability to provide self-help, or to mobilize resources on his or her own behalf. Statistics indicate that the police are most often called upon to help and intervene on behalf of those who are least competent to provide for themselves: the poor, minority group members, the elderly, juveniles, battered spouses and so forth. If police officers make personal decisions to distribute protection to those who are most "deserving" of it, or most "worthwhile" to society, they will inevitably deny services to those who are most in need of them—even if they seem least deserving of them. In this instance, the fact that your prisoner was handcuffed and thus totally incapable of defending himself from harm only makes your partner's assault on him a more glaring violation of police responsibilities. For this reason, it may be that you have no choice but to accept the burdens of the next proposed option.

OPTION B: *Tell the truth in any event, regardless of peer pressure, your partner's wishes or your own material interest in covering up the truth.*

Telling the truth in this instance has a number of virtues. First, it provides the possibility of justice for the accuser in this case, your partner's victim. At least, then, the molester could have a fair trial in the sense of a truthful airing of his grievance; that is, the social contract could be upheld and the legal system could operate as intended.

Telling the truth may carry with it a special value because, both in court and the departmental hearing, you will be testifying under oath. An oath obligates you to affirm publicly and for the record that you are telling the truth. For a religious person or one who feels that one's word represents one's reputation, lying under oath severely compromises one's sense of self. Additionally, if you lie to protect yourself, knowing you have done the wrong thing, you jeopardize the possibility of enjoying your work or deriving satisfaction from it in the future. Finally, if it seems clear to the judge that you are telling a lie to cover for your partner, your credibility in future cases and the credibility of police as witnesses in general may be impaired. Some judges have been known to refuse to allow certain officers to testify in their courtrooms because they lacked credibility as witnesses, and some juries have been known to have acquitted guilty parties because of their inability to believe that the police were testifying truthfully against them. Put another way, in pursuit of saving your partner's or your own hide in this case, you might place your own future effectiveness as a witness—and thus as a police officer—in jeopardy. The use of a questionable means (lying) to achieve a short-term end (helping your partner) might undermine the longer-term end (fighting crime, convicting wrongdoers) for which you originally took the job.

It is also possible that telling the truth about your partner's abusive handling of the child molester might not get him into as much trouble as you would expect. Even if the jury found for the plaintiff, it might choose to award him only a token amount or no monetary damages at all. After all, it is unlikely that they will have a great deal of sympathy for him. Your partner's attorney is probably very capable of persuading the jurors that they might have acted similarly toward the plaintiff if they were in your partner's shoes. Besides, because the plaintiff is a child molester, his attorney probably has no intention of taking the case all the way to the courtroom, and is only using the threat of suing to extract a settlement from the police department and your partner before trial. He may in fact drop the whole matter rather than expose his client's character in open court. Thus, your willingness to go through with a trial may not be as great a threat to your partner as it first might appear.

Where your testimony could hurt your partner, more likely, is in the internal affairs investigation of his actions. Should the truth of his abuse of his prisoner be confirmed, your chief (or commissioner) might well think it obligatory to discipline your partner, even to the point of dismissing him from the department. Thus, even if you think the possibility of his losing in court is small, his career might still be jeopardized, if not terminated, by your telling the truth. Unless you think that he *deserves* dismissal for this abusive behavior, this would be a very heavy burden for both of you to bear. For you, the choice is between doing two "right" things with bad consequences: telling the truth (and so seeing him suffer the consequences of your honesty) or protecting him (and so compromising your integrity).

Again, one must take into account that some officers also think that, by telling the truth about your partner's actions, you could be placing your physical safety, even your survival, on the line. The code of loyalty is a form of group insurance meant to mitigate or compensate for some of the risks inherent in police work. Many officers see themselves as part of the "thin blue line" of individuals hired by respectable society to insulate civilization from the forces of chaos. In Joseph Wambaugh's term, police see themselves as the "new centurions," descendants of the legionnaires who guarded the Roman Empire's borders from the barbarians. This duty on the boundaries of respectable society makes police officers feel sometimes like a breed apart from their fellow citizens, mercenaries hired to do a dirty job who are thought of by "straight" folks as not quite fit to join in respectable company. Isolated from those with whom they identify and serve, yet contemptuous toward those they are hired to control, the new centurions stand alone, able to depend only on each other for understanding, support and backup in a crisis. More than one officer has told us things such as, "If we can't depend on each other, we can't depend on anyone," and a racially mixed class of police recruits once told us, "There aren't black officers and white officers; we're all one color: blue."

Because solidarity is thought literally to promote individual officer survival in the streets, breaking ranks can entail very serious risks to the individual officer. Without trying overly to dramatize this point, we note that a few (but not many) experienced officers have reported that they know of specific instances in which an officer in trouble who called for backup received no help or help that arrived at a lackadaisical pace, because he or she had violated the code of loyalty or solidarity in some way. One way to break the code is to fail to demonstrate physical courage in backing up a fellow officer.[6] Another is to "fink" or "rat" on a fellow officer, that is, to tell the truth about a colleague's "minor" misdeeds in such a way that it gets the fellow officer in legal or disciplinary difficulties. (Again, revealing his "grave" misdeeds—selling drugs, thieving in uniform—is more acceptable.) In this case, testifying on behalf of the child molester against your colleague would definitely fall in the category of "finking."

A question remains of whether the risk attendant upon telling the truth outweighs the injunction to tell it. If you "fink," your own effectiveness may be destroyed by your fellow officers, just as your effectiveness as a witness may be destroyed if you lie under oath. Further, finking may put your life unnecessarily at risk, which is unfair to your family or loved ones as well as yourself. After all, it was your partner and not you who committed the mistake of beating the prisoner. It was wrong of him to commit a clear breach of department rules and, possibly, the law. He was also wrong to write an inaccurate report of the incident. Yet, by telling the truth about his wrongdoing, it seems, you would be exposing yourself to as much risk or more than he is facing in this situation.

Some officers with whom we have discussed this hypothetical example have told us that they would resent having to choose between complicity in a crime and snitching on a partner, and that a "good" partner would tell the truth rather than implicate you or put you in such a difficult spot. This may be true, and having your partner step forward to resolve your dilemma would be ideal. However, the ideal does not always happen, and although we have heard this suggestion often in our training classrooms, and even heard officers say that they would not work with a partner who would put them in this situation, rarely can we assure ourselves that those to whom we are connected will never lose control or make mistakes in judgment. Denying that this could happen to you is no solution to the dilemma. Surely, not allowing him to get in the back seat with the molester would have gone a long way toward preventing your current dilemma, but events have now proceeded beyond recapturing that opportunity. Next time you will know better than to allow him this error; perhaps next time you will know better than to keep him as a partner. This time, perhaps there is a middle ground on which to stand in this dilemma. Let us see if the next option provides it.

OPTION C: *Ask your partner's permission to tell the truth. If he grants it, testify honestly and accurately. However, if he asks you to stick by the story in his report that the offender resisted arrest, go along with his wishes.*

This option might allow you to meet the formal requirements of honesty, since your partner might grant you permission to testify accurately, which would then exonerate you in the eyes of your colleagues if he suffered negative consequences. Perhaps a direct request from you will prompt him to do the right thing. Even if he does not let you off the hook, in the minds of some there might be something gained here. If you were compelled to meet the demands of loyalty, they argue, it would be because your partner explicitly invoked the group insurance policy by insisting that you lie on his behalf. In that case, they feel that your partner assumes the moral responsibility for your dishonesty. Under those circumstances, they think you might find it easier to live with the lie.

To be sure, the likelihood of your partner granting you the freedom to testify against him is remote: if he were not trying to cover up his actions, he would confess and there would be no need for you to testify. Clearly, all the objections to your willing cover-up of his actions would still come into play. Option C, then, appears to be not very different from Option A, other than that you could rationalize that deception was offered on someone else's request rather than voluntarily, a rather unconvincing excuse. Perhaps, then, we need to look at the final option in our search for a choice that protects you from directly denying the truth of the molester's allegations against your partner.

OPTION D: *Tell the court and investigators a partial truth: stick to the false story that the offender resisted arrest, but acknowledge that your partner violated regulations by traveling in the back seat with him. Justify this decision by asserting that the offender seemed depressed, that you were worried that he might inflict harm on himself and your partner's riding in the back seemed the best preventive to self-mutilative behaviors. Claim that you do not know what happened in the back seat because you were driving the car and paying attention to the road and your police radio, and that you assume that the offender's injuries must have been sustained when he struggled to resist arrest.*

This option basically tries to avoid testifying to the benefit of either side. Saying that you did not detect any foul play in the back seat neither affirms nor denies your partner's guilt; it merely says that you did not see anything. It avoids your directly affirming the complainant's story without denying its possible accuracy. This solution has the advantage of neutrality: you have neither helped the accuser nor defended your partner.

However, it has its disadvantages. For one thing, it is a lie told under oath; you do know that your partner beat the child molester. Thus, your neutrality is incomplete, since withholding the truth benefits your partner more than it benefits his accuser. You are depriving the child molester of justice in his case against your partner. You are condoning violence against secured prisoners. You are telling your partner that you approve of his actions or at least do not condemn them. Surely, gratuitous violence by the police is unacceptable in each and every case, even if the failure to inflict it means that offenders may not, in your judgment, receive sufficient (and in some cases, any) punishment.

From the point of view of the police code of the streets, Option D may fail to live up to the standards of loyalty. Your failure to back up your partner's story completely may provide an opening through which a judge or jury could find reason to doubt your partner's story. Placing him in the back seat of the car could be very damaging to his defense. Given that a jury or judge is likely to expect your complete concordance in your stories, your failure to testify that the molester sustained his injuries while resisting arrest might well be interpreted as confirmation that his account is basically true and that your partner's story is a lie. In short, your "neutral" stance might well be interpreted as pro-molester.

Put another way, a neutral position may not be possible in this instance. You will have lied and compromised your own integrity and still not have done your partner any good by your actions, thus earning you the worst of both worlds. In the end, there may be no fully satisfactory option to this dilemma, in the sense of leaving you with a clear conscience, your partner off the hook and your colleagues thinking that you are a "stand up cop." Police work, like other morally challenging professions, sometimes calls on its practitioners to decide among poor and worse choices. In this case, telling the truth may turn out to be both the right and the most painful thing to do. Unfortunately, pain brings no exemption from having to make a best choice in this scenario.

Recently, the authors have been part of a police training agency task force that designed a state-wide ethics curriculum. One of our colleagues on the project, a veteran police officer and trainer, suggested that a value central to all police ethical performance is "courage." By courage, he meant the willingness to take personal risks to one's safety on behalf of others. These risks are voluntarily assumed and inherent in the obligations an officer assumes by swearing the oath of office. Although they are paid to take risks, the officers' salaries, by themselves, do not purchase the officers' courage. When officers voluntarily take avoidable risks and even lose their lives protecting others, it is because they believe that risk-taking is a moral obligation under the social contract, and not simply a condition of the employment contract.

Officers who tell the truth at great potential personal cost also take risks. Speaking out against a fellow officer's professional misconduct on behalf of principles such as truthfulness, individual rights and the due process of law, even if the beneficiaries of that risk-taking appear to be "unworthy" individuals, can entail great personal sacrifice to the officer who "blows the whistle." It would be glib to conclude with the thought that the truth-teller ultimately and always benefits when his or her honor and integrity remain intact. Ostracism by other officers can be painful and, possibly, dangerous. How does one measure the benefit of integrity against the burden of ostracism? There are no scales that will weigh these consequences and determine a clear balance. In some circumstances, say a deep undercover operation, maintaining the trust of one's colleagues may, in fact, be more important than maintaining one's integrity, at least in the face of immediate threat or danger. This cannot be known in advance, and it is a judgment each officer must make in the heat of action. In some departments, it may indeed be too risky to go against a strong tide of lying and deceit.

Nevertheless, according to the standards of ethical police work as we have outlined them, officers should tell the truth in the case we have been examining (that is, they *should* choose Option B). The value of having standards, it seems to us, is that they provide benchmarks against which we can measure ourselves and our character. As a practical matter, however, living up to the benchmarks at times will entail great risk and struggle. We cannot simply condemn those who fail to meet a difficult standard, but we can save our admiration of those who try to live up to it. The next chapter explains why the risk and struggle are, in the end, worthwhile.

NOTES

1. Of course, police work is assigned and reviewed by administrators and supervisors but, in the main, officers on patrol or responding to calls for assistance are usually not directly supervised as they perform their field work.

2. See, for example, Paul Chevigny, *Police Power* (New York: Pantheon Books, 1969), pp. 136–46.

3. The parallel with other professionals having responsibility for each other's malpractice should be obvious here: bar associations investigate and review the conduct of attorneys, physicians' groups such as state medical societies investigate medical malpractice allegations and, in many states, judicial review boards composed of sitting judges review complaints against their peers.

4. William A. Westley, *Violence and the Police* (Cambridge, Mass.: M.I.T. Press, 1970).

5. On permissible and impermissible police lies, see Edwin J. Delattre, *Character and Cops* (Washington, D.C.: American Enterprise Institute for Public Policy Research, 1989), pp. 160–66.

6. Joseph Wambaugh's *The Onion Field* (New York: Dell, 1973) presents a classic example of this when, during roll call, a Los Angeles Police Department captain blamed Officer Karl Hettinger for giving up his gun and thus "letting" his partner, Ian Campbell, get killed.

Conclusion

Our concern in this book has been to articulate a moral perspective for evaluating police behavior and to apply that perspective to a number of typical cases that police are likely to encounter in the course of their work. Since this concern falls within the domain of ethics, its proper focus has been on the question: What is the right thing for police to do? Because this is a question of ethics rather than social science, we are well aware that its answer is not to be found in an examination of actual police practices. In the language of ethics, this is a prescriptive rather than a descriptive inquiry. It is focused on what police *should* do rather than on how they actually behave in the kinds of situations we have described. If it is clear, for example, that police should not, from a moral point of view, accept gratuities, then the "fact" (if it is a fact) that a great majority of officers in America have accepted a gratuity at one time or another cannot change the moral proposition. We are not saying that the "wrongness" of taking gratuities is completely clear-cut or that officers commonly take them. Our point here is that widespread practice, entrenched custom or the dictates of police culture do not, by themselves, establish a moral standard. If a moral principle is correct, it is correct even though people rarely, if ever, live up to it.

There is some comfort in knowing that our moral standards are more enduring than current practice. Morality must have more substance and less transience than fashion if it is to see us through the difficult and wrenching experiences that we sometimes face in life. However, even as we say this, we recognize that there is a danger in insulating our standards too much from the tests of custom and practice. The risk here is that the standards may not seem relevant to police work if the decisions and actions of police officers never appear to take them into account.

If morality is too far removed from practice, it cannot be a guide in difficult times. A standard that is unreachable by most people most of the time is not only unhelpful, but it is suspect. Morality, after all, is meant to guide the actions of humans, not angels. There must come a time in our thinking about a standard that is rarely met when we stop questioning the behavior that does not meet it and begin questioning the standard itself. We are not saying that such a standard could not be correct if it was widely regarded as irrelevant. Our point here is that when people's practices diverge widely from a standard of behavior we need to reconsider the standard as well as the practice. Of course, there have been moments in history when groups of people were so corrupt that their behavior bore no relation to any moral standards we might apply to them. This might be said of groups that practiced human sacrifice, engaged in genocide, kept slaves or murdered civilians in war. However, since we maintain that the standards we have articulated are relevant measures for police action and behavior, we do not think that American police in general could be charged with such gross corruption or immorality today. For the most part, police organizations and individual officers acknowledge the values inherent in the standards we have put forward. To the extent that there is reluctance in the police world to embrace these standards, it may be that the standards seem too exacting or too inflexible to acknowledge "justifiable" exemptions that may be required for practical reasons in individual cases.

ETHICAL VERSUS "STREETWISE" BEHAVIOR

Every work in applied ethics must eventually come to grips with the question of its relevance to practitioners. The issue here is not whether police currently think of their work in the ways described in this book, but rather whether these ideas and ways of thinking about police work could help police to do their jobs better. Here we mean not more efficiently, but more in accord with our society's values and expectations of police.

For this to be so, police would have to accept the idea that their work could be better in a moral sense if they *attempted* to meet these standards than if they ignored them in difficult situations. In other words, police would have to accept the idea that abandoning the standards in a given situation was a moral shortfall rather than simply a more practical approach to the job. The threat to the relevance of ethics for police is not just individual officer brutality or corruption (as is widely assumed, even in police training); it is also "pragmatics"—the view that ethics is relevant only in the academy, whereas actual practice is judged by the standard of what is "streetwise."[1] Good police work, from the streetwise perspective, need not conform to any of the values we have articulated as long as officers can "handle" situations without being disciplined for violating department rules or creating a public scandal that brings negative publicity. Elements of the streetwise approach include a wide range of behaviors: the relatively small things in the streetwise officer's view (searching out merchants that give "police discounts" or free merchandise, finding good places to sleep while on duty), cutting corners (lying about the identity of informants when seeking a search warrant, classifying a call as unfounded rather than taking the time and effort to write a report about a street fight or other minor incident), controlling one's beat (using unnecessary force to intimidate those persons least likely to file a complaint, filing charges for resisting arrest against those whom the officer feels might file a brutality charge against him) and so on. Streetwise policing can save the officer effort in keeping peace on the streets and money in that he pays less for the out-of-pocket expenses associated with going to work. Performing in streetwise ways can also help an officer become and stay accepted by his more experienced colleagues. In policing, as in other professions, sharing knowledge of the more secretive and somewhat shameful practices of colleagues can create a bond among practitioners that builds loyalty and a sense of belonging.

What we are calling the streetwise alternative to ethics for police has its attractions—particularly where police work is not readily visible to most of society. This orientation toward policing is often associated with vice work or working on skid row, where police are regularly dealing with an isolated and socially scorned population, and where living up to the moral standards makes results difficult to achieve.[2] In these and similar circumstances, the "streetwise" alternative to ethics—entrapment, evidence plants, perjury, inflicting pain on uncooperative persons—may seem less frustrating to the officer who wants to control potentially violent or lawbreaking individuals.

Beyond the attraction of results, this approach to policing may be enforced on new officers by those already working in that mode. When a field training officer says to a new recruit "forget what you learned in the academy; this is how it is done on the street," he is doing more than giving an opinion. The recruit is being put on notice that he must accept local police customs and practices—to play by the rules of the department's culture or risk being an outsider, with all that implies for isolation (or worse).

CAN OFFICERS LIVE UP TO THE STANDARDS?

This dilemma for the new officer in a squad shows that the question of the relevance of ethical standards to police work has two parts: First, is it possible for officers to accept, and act in accordance with, such standards in their work? Second, is there anything to commend the acceptance of these standards over the "streetwise" approach to the job?

When we turn to the possibility of an officer adopting the standards and trying to live up to them, we must recognize that it leads down a well-traveled road in moral philosophy. Our first question echoes Immanuel Kant's attempt to demonstrate that human beings can be held to moral standards based on our experience with moral judgments.[3] When he set out to explore the foundations of human morality, Immanuel Kant realized that we must begin with the basic assumption that people are in a position to make a free choice of a moral course over an immoral one. If that choice is not open to us, it is senseless to say that the person who followed the immoral course "ought" to have done otherwise. A moral requirement may not be imposed where people have literally no chance to meet it. Applying this rule to our case, we may say: if it is truly impossible for an officer to pursue police work in accordance with the five standards we have articulated, then the standards should be rejected as irrelevant to that officer's practice. Although Kant was concerned with free choice at a very abstract level, we would accept this point in regard to the officer's options in day-to-day activity. To explore this question seriously, we must acknowledge that the possibility of meeting these standards depends upon three factors: an individual's understanding, intention and environment.

The practical ingredients an individual needs in order to have free moral choice in matters of professional conduct are an understanding of the values that inform his or her profession, the intention to live up to the values and an environment that supports those values and discourages behavior that is contrary to them. Where these three factors are present, it is not only possible, but often likely, that officers will live up to the standards we are proposing. Our immediate concern, however, has to do with the consequences of an absence of these factors or their presence in limited forms. To the extent that they are weak or not present in the officer's world, the possibility of a relevant ethics for his or her work is more difficult to sustain.

The first factor, understanding, is clearly the major one addressed in this work. We have systematically defined a moral perspective that is the conceptual foundation of the American form of government, one that is widely shared by the American populace. We have, further, used that perspective to derive a specific set of responsibilities for police as government officials, that is, the five standards. Finally, we applied those standards to the kinds of situations that police are likely to face and that raise moral questions for them. All of this can contribute to an officer's understanding of police work. The function of our work parallels the function of academy training in ethics. Typically in academy ethics training, the values of the department or agency are spelled out in either a code of ethics, a departmental statement of its values or, at a minimum, the rules and regulations governing "conduct unbecoming an officer." Training, then, generally consists of reviewing or explaining these values statements, and in the more progressive departments, of applying them through discussion to examples of actual police conduct.

Recently, some police organizations have begun to enunciate and explain publicly the values they espouse. One might argue about how well this is done or how much conviction stands behind instruction in ethical standards; we are not saying that such training is extensive, consistent or even always sincere. Until quite recently, ethics was not even a part of police training, nor were officers encouraged to distinguish between a moral and a legal standard of behavior. Nevertheless, police do not come to their work from a moral vacuum. They bring to it their own moral training, their common moral sense and their desire to make a social contribution. Moreover, there are a number of police codes of ethics that have been officially adopted by national and state training agencies and by local departments. These are generally circulated to recruits in academy training and reproduced in policy manuals. At varying levels of appreciation, it is fair to say that most police officers understand the values that inform their profession. Whether they understand them well enough to make decisions and take action in light of them is, perhaps, another matter. Our interest here, however, is in the possibility of such decision-making and action. For practical purposes, police seem to understand their moral responsibilities well enough to feel bound by them, if only to avoid punishment for violating departmental rules governing their conduct. In other words, the first condition for free moral choices by a police officer—understanding—can be met by virtually all officers.

The second factor is the intention to live up to a moral standard. This is the factor that is most under the control of the individual officer, or at least this is the factor for which he or she is most personally accountable. We believe that most people who choose police work do so out of a desire to serve others. Policing is not a profession that particularly attracts those looking for wealth or gratitude. Historically, it has been an occupation of upward mobility and (paradoxically, given its dangers) security. It does not seem to attract people who are significantly more vicious or greedy than other professions, though no doubt such types find their way into uniform. Surveying the police profession on the whole, it is fair to say that those who enter it are not substantially better or worse intentioned than other well-meaning people. So, although there may be officers who have no desire to live up to ethical standards, there is nothing about the profession that preferentially selects its prospects for that trait. Indeed, the "protect and serve" orientation of modern police work may, if anything, encourage the well-intentioned.

In the end, it is the third factor, the work environment, that is a major determinant of whether it will be possible for those officers who understand the ethical standards and have the desire to meet them to do so. There is no general and clear-cut answer to the question of whether it is possible to meet these standards because officers work in different and changing environments. Vice work in a major urban center is a different world from patrolling a middle-class residential suburb. Each department has its own orientation toward the values inherent in the social contract. Where this orientation is insular, monolithic and self-protecting, there may be little chance for an officer to act with independent moral judgment. The world of Frank Serpico, in which by his account nearly all his New York Police Department colleagues were "on the take" and the department's administration refused to confront this fact, represents an extreme environment in which the possibility and relevance of moral action are diminished. William Westley described another department that was an extremely closed, constrained workplace. On the other hand, a department with a progressive chief and a sturdy structure of accountability (the department Muir describes in *Police: Streetcorner Politicians*, for example) makes the application of ethical standards to police behavior both relevant and pressing.

Most officers work in environments that are more mixed in their support of ethical standards. Many departments have not tried very systematically to build a consensus of shared values, or they have left the department culture to evolve from unwritten custom and inertia. Some departments are split, housing both moral cynics and moral zealots in an uneasy balance of power. New officers in such departments may find that their choice between ethics and streetwise practices has political overtones that will very greatly affect their friendships and working relationships in the department. In yet other departments, the moral perspective of the field training officer or the squad supercedes the departmental moral environment for the new officer.

One thing that is clear is that the care and nurturing of a receptive environment are extremely important for making ethical standards relevant to police work. If a department takes these standards seriously and holds officers accountable for them, it will close the gap between ethics and pragmatics—the wise and the streetwise. If a department does not give this issue much attention, the moral burden will fall to the individual officer. To the extent that a department *actively and systematically discourages* moral behavior, the officer may feel he has an excuse for not living up to society's moral expectations. Such a department, however, would be a rare case. In any event, many officers are not willing to so easily let themselves off the moral hook. Joseph Wambaugh's *The Onion Field* explores the psyche of an officer who cannot rid himself of guilt feelings over having not saved his partner's life. Frank Serpico managed to maintain his deepest principles even in the face of explicit threats to his safety. Police fiction provides additional stirring examples of individual officers' moral courage, but there are countless other real-life examples of police swimming against the tide and taking the consequences. We concede that living up to moral standards can be difficult in an environment that is indifferent or hostile to them. Still, moral behavior does not seem to be impossible, even in extremely inhospitable environments. There may be small comfort in knowing this, but our point has to do with the possibility of morality, not its ease.

Any compassionate person would judge less harshly an officer who failed to live up to these standards in a non-supportive environment, but we would first make the negative judgment before tempering it. Were the officer acting in a world where living up to the standards was not possible, we would have no business making the negative judgment at all. In that world, ethical standards would be truly irrelevant; "streetwise" would be all we could expect. However, short of that extreme, the streetwise approach runs the risk of being nothing more than an easy way to avoid responsibility for one's actions.

BENEFITS OF LIVING UP TO THE STANDARDS

It is clear, then, that the ethical standards *can* apply to police work as we know it. However, is there any reason to believe that police officers should *prefer* those standards to the streetwise approach to their jobs? Can we commend them to the police, and on what grounds? This question calls up one of the oldest challenges to ethics: can there be more to morality than the advantages it may happen to bring to a person? This is Thrasymacus's challenge to Socrates in Plato's *Republic*,[4] and philosophers have been wrestling with it ever since. Is morality to be followed only as long as one thinks it is in one's interest? This is the core of the streetwise mentality. Plato set out to show that morality (justice) is of value not only for its apparent benefits, but in itself (despite any appearances to the contrary).

It is puzzling to think about how we might go about recommending morality to those who are likely to challenge or abandon it when conformity to moral standards is not convenient. The appeal to accept moral standards in such circumstances can hardly rest on a yet deeper moral foundation. If the challenger accepted that foundation, he would never express these doubts in the first place. Once expressed, the appeal to another level of morality simply invites a repeat of the challenge at that new level. We have here the makings of an infinite regress of moral appeal and moral skepticism. How can we commend morality to the doubtful if we know in advance that we cannot base our recommendation on what is inherently "good" or what "ought" to be done?

In order to meet the doubts about moral standards for police as they arise from the perspective of the streetwise, it is often useful to begin the debate on the ground of self-interest. After all, what the streetwise cop has to offer the new recruit is efficiency, effectiveness, minimizing of risk to oneself and, perhaps, profit—the makings of self-interest. In pursuing this line of thought, we do not mean to suggest that nothing more than this can be said on morality's behalf. However, in our experience, the appeal of the streetwise perspective is very powerful, particularly to recent recruits. It is worth taking some time to examine its value—even on its own terms. To do so, let us pose the following question: Is there any reason to believe that adopting the moral standards we have identified and trying to act in accordance with them could be *more* in an officer's *self-interest* than the streetwise alternative?

We think that there are some reasons to believe this is so. In the first place, the appeal of the streetwise approach to policing depends upon the absence of counterpressure to conform to moral standards. In departments with strong internal disciplinary units or a chief committed to enforcing rules and regulations, going along with a streetwise culture carries its own risks. They may be less immediate, but they can ultimately be serious. Officers have lost pay and even their jobs when their failure to act in accordance with official standards of behavior has been established.

In recent years, some departments have been moved to establish training programs in ethics on the advice of legal counsel. Their concerns have revolved around complex questions of civil liability for an officer's actions. If an officer is sued in civil court for excessive use of force or some other behavior that has harmed a civilian, a question arises as to whether the officer or the department is liable. Some departments have become concerned that an officer who loses such a suit might, in turn, sue the department for the value of the judgment on the grounds that the department did not train the officer to behave properly in that situation (and thus avoid harming the civilian). In order to forestall this possibility, those departments have developed training programs in ethics and required all of their officers to attend them. Above and beyond whatever noble intent such departments might have in establishing ethics courses, they have also established a basis for denying their own liability for an officer's improper actions, should the issue arise in court.

The effect of departmental precaution in the area of ethics training is to expose the streetwise practices of some officers to individual (rather than departmental) liability. The streetwise officer may act in the uniform of a public servant, but by violating the department's standards, he or she takes risks as a private individual. This seems to us to shift the balance of self-interest toward adherence to departmental standards. An officer who can demonstrate in a civil suit that she or he was following approved policy, acting on training instructions or behaving in accordance with official statements of values is likely to retain the department as an umbrella of liability protection. Given the stakes in civil liability suits, this is a significant counterweight to the claims of efficiency and minimizing of daily hassles that are among the attractions of streetwise policing.

MORALITY AND JOB SATISFACTION

There is also a less monetary conception of self-interest that argues for the moral standards against the streetwise perspective. Muir[5] tries to discern the difference between officers who grow and develop in their jobs and those who "burn out." He proposes that the difference is ultimately grounded in the officer's personal moral attitudes. Muir classifies officers' moral attitudes according to their views about human nature and their views about the use of force. Officers with a "tragic perspective" on human nature see others as they see themselves and recognize what all people have in common. Officers with a "cynical perspective" on human nature tend to emphasize the irreconcilable differences between "good" people and "bad" people. They see the world in terms of "us versus them" and have little compassion for "them." Officers also must come to terms with the role of force in their work. Those who "integrate" the wise use of necessary force in their moral scheme recognize its value for keeping the public safe from those who would harm them. Others are, in Muir's term, "conflicted" about the use of force and regard the need for it as a moral failing— however necessary it might be in some instances. In Muir's study, officers who have a tragic perspective and an integrated understanding of the use of force are most likely to enjoy their work and be good at it. Muir calls these officers "professionals," and notes that they are widely admired in their departments.

Although it is true that Muir studied officers in a department that tried to hold them accountable to a high standard of behavior, it is also persuasive that the job is hard enough without the isolation that comes with being a breed apart. Officers who follow practices that are illegal or that have no approval in the wider community, even if they are tolerated within their departments, are driven into a brotherhood that can shut them off from the full range of benefits of social living. It does not seem plausible to think it is in the officer's self-interest to live only in a small circle of fellow officers. To the extent that this diminished world is created and maintained by the streetwise approach to policing, that approach is not of longer-term benefit to the officers who pursue it—despite the day-to-day advantages of cutting corners.

Finally, if police work is to be professionally satisfying, the satisfaction is most likely to come from that part of the job that involves decision-making rather than the routine implementation of policy. Much of police work is discretionary, and discretion provides the opportunity for creativity in work. There are two major elements in the use of discretion: the range of authority and the exercise of judgment.

In order to use their discretion properly, police officers must be aware of which judgments are theirs to make. They must understand where their actions are specified in policy or law, such as when a warrant is needed to conduct a search, and where their actions are open to their own choices, such as when to cite a motorist for rolling through a stop sign without coming to a full stop. This is the understanding of the officer's range of authority.

Within the boundaries of their authority, officers are able to make choices about how to do their work. Officers are often in a position to set their own priorities concerning the use of their time, and they are more often in a position to select the best means to accomplish their purposes. These decisions call for judgment, and the judgments they make will have consequences—for good or for ill. A decision about how to resolve a family dispute can provide a framework for reconciliation (or protection) of spouses and children, or it can end in violence and pain. The officer has authority to act in a variety of ways and has enough options to act foolishly or wisely. This is a challenge of the job that carries benefits as well as risks. The risk, of course, is accountability and blame should one's decision turn out badly. It may seem easier to avoid discretion in order to pass the blame for failures up the line, but apart from the fact that discretion is not easily avoided, its benefits are accountability and, hopefully, praise. The other side of the risk of exercising discretion is the chance for recognition of one's own good judgment. Wise or courageous actions are a credit, in the first instance, to the individual officer who uses discretion well. If the department deserves any credit, it is for training and nurturing the wise use of discretion in its officers and for recognizing their accomplishments.

Although there are some departments that may not sincerely value officer discretion, much less its wise use, in the end it is, nonetheless, up to each officer to find ways to make decisions made in the course of police work personally and professionally satisfying. Even in an atmosphere of departmental cynicism where the watchwords are "go along to get along," each officer must take some responsibility for the department's and his performance. The officer who wants more from the job must either buck the tide of cynicism or find another line of work. Those are individual choices. Our point is that the wise exercise of discretion is not always easy, but it is a major component of job satisfaction, and it is up to the individual officer to pursue it.

The responsibility for accepting, and acting in accordance with, the moral standards we have described is the officer's. The fact that this will be difficult or risky in some departments, or in certain situations in any department, is undeniable, but that does not make these standards irrelevant in those departments or those situations. It makes action in accordance with them difficult or risky. On the other side, it is the possibility of risk that makes moral action courageous and admirable. If it were easy to live up to moral standards, we would all be heroes. Although that might be better for the world, it would not do much for heroism. In a sense, police work is interesting and satisfying because it is morally perilous.

Most people do not have so many opportunities to live a life of moral courage. Police may feel they have a surplus of such opportunities. They may even feel burdened by them. Nevertheless, police work is not just another job. Society's street-level referees have certain obligations to those they police—obligations they may not set aside for an easier day. If those obligations lead to difficulties or even to moral crises, that is to be expected and, to some degree, welcomed. However, it would be a loss to dismiss those opportunities to the category of irrelevancy for the sake of a streetwise approach to the job. Those officers who seek satisfaction in their work really have no choice but to acknowledge the moral standards of their profession and meet them to the best of their ability.

NOTES

1. Academy instructors are acutely aware that their teachings are often undermined when new recruits hit the street. Many instructors take this issue up

directly with recruits in the academy and discuss it openly in order to prepare them for the conflict. Unfortunately, advice in this area may sound self-serving when it comes only from an academy instructor and not from officers on the street.

2. Jonathan Rubinstein, *City Police* (New York: Ballantine Books, 1973), pp. 376–402.

3. Immanuel Kant, *Groundwork of the Metaphysic of Morals* (New York: Harper Torchbooks, 1964).

4. Plato, *The Republic* (Baltimore: Penguin Books, 1955), pp. 62–77.

5. William Ker Muir, Jr., *Police: Streetcorner Politicians* (Chicago: University of Chicago Press, 1977), p. 224.

Bibliography

Armstrong, Terry R. and Kenneth M. Cinnamon (eds.). *Power and Authority in Law Enforcement*. Springfield, Ill.: Charles C. Thomas, 1976.

Banton, Michael. *The Police in the Community*. New York: Basic Books, 1964.

Berlin, Isaiah. "Two Concepts of Liberty." *Four Essays on Liberty*. Oxford, England: Oxford University Press, 1969.

Bittner, Egon. *The Functions of Police in Modern Society*. Washington, D.C.: U.S. Government Printing Office, 1967.

Brown, Michael. *Working the Street*. New York: Russell Sage Foundation, 1981.

Caplan, Gerald C. *ABSCAM Ethics: Moral Issues and Deception in Law Enforcement*. Cambridge, Mass.: Ballinger Publishing Company for the Police Foundation, 1983.

Chevigny, Paul. *Police Power*. New York: Pantheon Books, 1969.

Cohen, Howard. "Exploiting Police Authority." *Criminal Justice Ethics*, 2, no. 2, Summer/Fall, 1986.

———. "Working Ethics for Police Officers." *Criminal Justice Ethics*, 1, no. 1, Winter/Spring, 1982.

——— and Michael Feldberg. *Ethics for Professional Policing*. Harvard, Mass.: Wasserman Associates, 1985.

Davis, Kenneth Culp. *Discretionary Justice: A Preliminary Inquiry*. Urbana, Ill.: University of Illinois Press, 1971.

"Declaration of Independence." In Edward Conrad Smith (ed.), *The Constitution of the United States, with Case Summaries*, pp. 27–31. New York: Harper and Row, 1974.

Delattre, Edwin J. *Character and Cops*. Washington, D.C.: American Enterprise Institute for Public Policy Research, 1989.

Elliston, Frederick A. *Teaching Police Ethics*. Washington, D.C.: Police Foundation, 1984.

———— and Michael Feldberg (eds.). *Moral Issues in Police Work*. Totowa, N.J.: Rowman and Allanheld, 1985.

Feldberg, Michael. "Gratuities, Corruption and the Democratic Ethos of Policing: The Case of the Free Cup of Coffee." In Frederick A. Elliston and Michael Feldberg (eds.), *Moral Issues in Police Work*, pp. 267–76. Totowa, N.J.: Rowman and Allanheld, 1985.

Felkenes, George T. and Harold K. Becker (eds.). *Law Enforcement: A Selected Bibliography*. Metuchen, N.J.: Scarecrow Press, 1977.

Fogelson, Robert. *Big-City Police*. Cambridge, Mass.: Harvard University Press, 1977.

Fuller, Lon L. *The Morality of Law*, revised ed. New Haven: Yale University Press, 1969.

Geller, William A. (ed.). *Police Leadership in America*. New York: Praeger, 1985.

Goldstein, Herman. *Policing a Free Society*. Cambridge, Mass.: Ballinger, 1977.

Hamilton, Alexander, James Madison and John Jay. *The Federalist Papers*. New York: New American Library of World Literature, 1961.

Heffernan, William C. and Timothy Stroup. *Police Ethics: Hard Choices in Law Enforcement*. New York: John Jay Press, 1985.

Hill, Christopher. *The Century of Revolution 1603–1714*. New York: Norton, 1961.

Hobbes, Thomas. *Leviathan*. New York: E. P. Dutton, 1950.

Kant, Immanuel. *Groundwork of the Metaphysic of Morals*. New York: Harper Torchbooks, 1964.

Kelling, George, Tony Pate, Duane Dieckman and Charles E. Brown. *The Kansas City Preventive Patrol Experiment: A Summary Report*. Washington, D.C.: Police Foundation, 1974.

Klockars, Carl A. *Thinking About Police*. New York: McGraw-Hill, 1983.

Locke, John. *Two Treatises of Civil Government: A Critical Edition with an Introduction and Apparatus Criticus*. Peter Laslett (ed.). Cambridge, England: Cambridge University Press, 1970.

Maas, Peter. *Serpico*. New York: Viking Press, 1973.

Marx, Gary T. *Undercover: Police Surveillance in America*. Berkeley and Los Angeles: University of California Press, 1988.

————. "Who Really Gets Stung? Some Issues Raised by the New Undercover Work." In Frederick A. Elliston and Michael Feldberg (eds.), *Moral Issues in Police Work*. Totowa, N.J.: Rowman and Allanheld, 1985, pp. 99–127.

Muir, William Ker, Jr. *Police: Streetcorner Politicians*. Chicago: University of Chicago Press, 1977.

Plato. *The Republic*. Baltimore: Penguin Books, 1955.

Reiman, Jeffrey H. "The Social Contract and the Police Use of Deadly Force." In Frederick A. Elliston and Michael Feldberg (eds.), *Moral Issues in Police Work*, pp. 237–49. Totowa, N.J.: Rowman and Allanheld, 1985.

Rossiter, Clinton (ed.). *The Federalist Papers*. New York: New American Library, 1961.

Rubinstein, Jonathan. *City Police*. New York: Ballantine Books, 1973.

Sherman, Lawrence W. "Becoming Bent: Moral Careers of Corrupt Policemen." In Frederick A. Elliston and Michael Feldberg (eds.), *Moral Issues in Police Work*, pp. 253–65. Totowa, N.J.: Rowman and Allanheld, 1985.

———. *Ethics in Criminal Justice Education*. Hastings-on-Hudson: The Hastings Center, 1982.

———. *Police Corruption: A Sociological Perspective*. Garden City: Anchor Books, 1974.

——— and Richard A. Berk. "The Minneapolis Domestic Violence Experiment." *Police Foundation Reports* 1 (April, 1984), pp. 1–8.

Silberman, Charles E. *Criminal Violence, Criminal Justice*. New York: Vintage Books, 1980.

Skolnick, Jerome H. "Deception by Police." In Frederick A. Elliston and Michael Feldberg (eds.). *Moral Issues in Police Work*, pp. 75–99. Totowa, N.J.: Rowman and Allanheld, 1985.

———. *Justice Without Trial*. New York: John Wiley, 1966.

——— and Thomas C. Gray. *Police in America*. Boston: Little, Brown and Company, 1975.

Smith, Edward Conrad (ed.), *The Constitution of the United States, with Case Summaries*. New York: Harper and Row, 1974.

Wambaugh, Joseph. *The Onion Field*. New York: Dell, 1973.

Westley, William A. *Violence and the Police*. Cambridge, Mass.: MIT Press, 1970.

Wilson, James Q. *Varieties of Police Behavior*. Cambridge, Mass.: Harvard University Press, 1968.

Index

About the Authors

HOWARD S. COHEN is Associate Provost and Associate Professor of Philosophy at the University of Massachusetts–Boston, where he has been Chairperson of the Philosophy Department and Director of the Law and Justice Program. Dr. Cohen has published in the areas of social philosophy and applied ethics. His previous works include *Equal Rights for Children* (1980) and several articles on police authority and police ethics. He taught police ethics in the Boston University Law Enforcement Trainers Institute and in the Institute for the Humanities and Law Enforcement Training of the National Association of State Directors of Law Enforcement Training.

MICHAEL FELDBERG is currently President of The Boston-Fenway Program, Inc., and Adjunct Professor of Urban Affairs and Criminal Justice at Metropolitan College, Boston University. He is the former Director of the Boston University Law Enforcement Trainers Institute and the Institute for the Humanities and Criminal Justice. He has taught at Northeastern University, John Jay College of Criminal Justice, the Boston University School of Medicine, the University of Massachusetts–Boston and the Institute for the Humanities and Law Enforcement Training. He is the co-editor of *Moral Issues in Police Work* (1985), and the author of two works in American history, *The Turbulent Era: Riot and Disorder in Jacksonian America* (1980) and *The Philadelphia Riots of 1844: A Study of Ethnic Conflict* (1975).

CPSIA information can be obtained
at www.ICGtesting.com
Printed in the USA
BVHW040034170419
545729BV00015B/108/P